A TABLE BEFORE ME

CONGREGATION BETH SHALOM SISTERHOOD
PITTSBURGH, PENNSYLVANIA

About Sisterhood

Congregation Beth Shalom Sisterhood is affiliated with The Women's League for Conservative Judaism. We are organized to further the preservation of traditional Judaism and recognizes that the home, the synagogue and its religious school, are necessary to reach these ideals. Important beneficiaries of our efforts include donations to the residence halls at the Jewish Theological Seminary, provides scholarships for high school Juniors to participate in Jewish programs, provides holiday packages for the residents of the Charles Morris Center. The ultimate goal for our membership is the ascending achievement in personal Jewish development and to express hope that our leadership will provide a paradigm for others to emulate. The proceeds from *A Table Before Me* go toward all these endeavors.

Additional copies may be obtained at the cost of $19.95,
plus $3.00 postage and handling, each book.

Send to:
Beth Shalom Sisterhood
5915 Beacon St.
Pittsburgh, PA 15217
412-421-2288

First Printing

ISBN 0-9711108-0-8

WIMMER
COOKBOOKS
ConsolidatedGraphics

1-800-548-2537

Introduction

More and more of us are choosing to dine at home with family or close friends. What easier way to plan a menu than to peruse the pages of a cookbook filled with favorite recipes of people who share common interests and tastes!

We are grateful that so many talented cooks shared their prized recipes with us. Some recipes are originals while others have been handed down from generation to generation. Most of these recipes come from the kitchens of members and friends of the Congregation Beth Shalom Sisterhood. The recipes were all lovingly "home tested" by the people who submitted them. We regret that we were unable to include many quality recipes which were submitted due to similarity or availability of space.

We hope that this cookbook will help you prepare delicious and exciting meals in your own kitchen. Join us and enjoy *A Table Before Me*.

Cookbook Committee

Project Director and Editor: Sheila Glasser

Associate Editors: Ruth Ganz Fargotstein, Marlene Gelman, Rachel Kalnicki, Nancy Neudorf, Marce Schwartz

Committee: Elaine Beck, Sarita Eisner, Rhonda Gelman Kelley, Judy Kornblith, Harriet Kruman, Barbara Oleinick, Elayne Rosen, Sharon Schwartz, Dee Selekman,

Computer Editor: Sally Samuels

Computer Programmer/Consultant: Linda Greenberg (E-mail: lag@nauticom.net)

Graphic Designers: T.L. Carr, Dan Duch, Brenda Edwards, Andrew Fenlock

Special Mention: Hannah Rosner Art Director, Art Institute of Pittsburgh

Special Acknowledgments

As an added bonus, we wish to thank the restaurants and food specialist who have contributed creative and thoughtful recipes that reflect the casual elegance that defines cooking today.

Richard Amster
Food Editor, *The Jewish Chronicle*

Benkovitz Seafoods

Cafe Sam

Harold Caplan
Congregation Beth Shalom Caterer

Chef Mark Castelli
Asiago

Jane Citron
Food Writer/Consultant/Teacher

Chef David Conley
Poli Restaurant

Lila Grushka Catering

Chef Peter Lauterbach
Bravo Franco

Le Mont

Suzanne Martinson
Food Editor, *Pittsburgh Post Gazette*

Chef Louis Moré
Moré

Rania Harris
Rania's Catering

Bob Schnarenberger
Paper Moon Chef Services

Chef Victor Tome
Union Grill

Table of Contents

The Holidays

The aura of the Jewish holidays adds further meaning to food selection and preparation. In addition to laws governing these holidays, tradition and custom over the years has reinforced their significance to us.

For **Shabbat**, the table is beautifully set and among the silver, candles, wine cups and dishes are two loaves of challah covered with a cloth. They are symbolic of the double portion of manna which was gathered by the Israelites in the desert on the eve of Shabbat. (Exodus 16:4,5) There is nothing more delicious than fresh, home baked challah!

Rosh Hashanah marks the Jewish New Year. The celebration begins with a festive holiday meal, rich in foods that symbolize sweetness, blessings and abundance. The challahs are round, like the continuous circle of life. Honey is used as a dip for apples and in challah, baked goods and tzimmes in symbolic hope of a sweet year.

Yom Kippur, the holiest day of the year, is a day for fasting. The post fast meal is often dairy, including smoked fishes, kugels and baked goods such as honey cake.

On **Sukkot,** we dine in the Sukkah, an outdoor structure. Seasonal fruits and vegetables make lovely decorations for the Sukkah as well as become part of the menu.

The calendar continues with **Hanukah,** the Festival of Lights. Many dishes are prepared with oil to commemorate the oil, that burned for eight days in the ancient temple of Jerusalem at the time of rededication. Favored foods are those fried in oil such as latkes of all varieties and sufganyot (donuts).

The holiday of **Purim** follows, celebrating the success of good overcoming evil. Traditional delicacies are Hamantaschen, triangular cakes filled with poppy seeds, fruit fillings or even chocolate. Kreplach. dough triangles filled with cheese or meat are also served. Both Hamantaschen and kreplach remind us of the shape of evil Haman's tri-cornered hat.

Passover is a time when certain foods are prohibited from our menu, including all foods containing leavening. We remember the exodus from Egypt, when in the hasty departure of the Israelites, there was no time for the bread to rise. We eat matzo and many traditional and modern dishes made with matzo products. These special recipes are numerous and are contained in a separate chapter of this book.

Dairy foods are preferred for **Shavuot,** especially popular are blintzes and kugels.

APPETIZERS

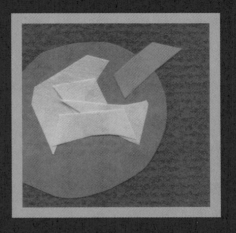

APPETIZERS

SPREADS AND DIPS

Baked Mock Crabmeat
  with Spinach and Cheese 9
Cream Cheese "Crab" Ball 10
Salmon Party Ball 11
Brie with Walnut Topping 11
Smoked Bluefish or
  Smoked Trout Pâté 12
Seven Layer Egg and
  Caviar Dazzler 12
Terrific Tantalizing Tuna Mousse 13
Layered Goat Cheese and Pesto 14
Lox Cheese Cake Appetizer 15
Grandma Ruth's Romanian
  Style Chopped Eggplant 16
Old-Fashioned Chopped Herring 16
Mock Chopped Liver 17
Spicy Dip 18
Tofu and Cauliflower Dip 18

OTHER

Gloria's Spicy Glazed Pecans 19
Portobello Mushrooms
  with Rosemary-Lime Marinade 20
Phyllo Champignon 21
Boursin Phyllo Tart 22
Potato Parsnip Pancakes
  with Smoked Salmon 23
Gravlax 24

Baked Mock Crabmeat with Spinach and Cheese

Delight family and friends with this delicious alternative to crabmeat. This is "the" recipe for that special gourmet touch.

1	**(10 ounce) package chopped frozen spinach, cooked, drained, dried**
1	**cup shredded cheese (cheese of your choice)**
2	**tablespoons minced onion**
6	**tablespoons butter or margarine, melted**
2	**tablespoons flour**
1	**cup milk**
1	**pound imitation crabmeat or lobster product, drained and flaked**
1	**tablespoon lemon juice**
1/8	**teaspoon curry powder (optional)**
1/2	**teaspoon salt**
3/4	**cup soft bread crumbs**
1/8	**teaspoon rosemary (optional)**

Arrange spinach in a greased 11 x 7-inch baking dish.
Sprinkle with cheese, set aside.
Cook onion in butter in saucepan over medium-high heat, stirring constantly.
Reduce heat to low, add flour, stirring until blended.
Add milk, cook 1 minute stirring constantly until thick and bubbly.
Stir in crabmeat, lemon juice, curry and salt.

Spoon fish mixture evenly over cheese.
Sprinkle with bread crumbs and rosemary.
Bake uncovered in 350 degree oven 30 minutes.
May be cooked and frozen.
Reheat in oven or microwave in pan of warm water.

Serves 6

Florie Krell

Cream Cheese "Crab" Ball

This impressive hors d'oeuvres is a favorite of mine. It was given to me by Richard Alderman of "The Crab House." Assembled the day before, it's perfect for a large crowd. The lively addition of horseradish is guaranteed to satisfy everyone's taste buds.

2	(8 ounce) packages cream cheese, softened (not whipped)
1	small onion, minced
1	teaspoon lemon juice
1	teaspoon garlic salt
2	teaspoons Worcestershire sauce
1/4	cup mayonnaise
2	teaspoons horseradish
2	(8 ounce) packages imitation crabmeat chunks, drained and flaked
1 1/2	(12 ounce) jars cocktail sauce

Combine everything except mock crabmeat and cocktail sauce, mix well.
Add 3 tablespoons cocktail sauce and mix well.
Cover and chill approximately 3 or 4 hours.

Place cream cheese on large piece of plastic wrap.
Flatten out to form a 12 x 7-inch rectangle.
Mix one package of crab with 3 tablespoons cocktail sauce.
Fill center of cream cheese with crab mixture.
Lift sides of wrap to help fold cream cheese over fish to form a ball.

Combine second package of crab with remaining cocktail sauce.
Roll ball in crab mixture, pressing softly to cover completely.
Cover with plastic wrap, chill overnight.
Serve with crackers and party rye.

Note: May add additional cocktail sauce over top as needed.

Serves 16

Sheila Glasser

Salmon Party Ball

Lots of toasted almonds, this creamy spread is thick and satisfying. It features salmon, cream cheese, liquid smoke and horseradish to give a nice zip.

1	(14 3/4 ounce) can salmon
1	(8 ounce) package cream cheese, softened
1	tablespoon lemon juice
2	teaspoons grated onion
1	teaspoon prepared horseradish
1/4	teaspoon salt
1/4	teaspoon liquid smoke (optional)
1/2	cup chopped pecans, toasted
3	tablespoons snipped parsley

Drain and flake salmon, remove skin and bones.
Combine all ingredients except pecans and parsley.
Mix thoroughly, chill overnight.

Combine pecans and parsley.
Shape salmon mixture into a ball.
Roll ball in nut mixture, chill well.
Serve with party rye or crackers.

Serves 8

Judy Kornblith

Brie with Walnut Topping

This is a simple appetizer that is meant to be eaten at leisure with a glass of great wine in the company of good friends.

1	(8 ounce) wheel of Brie
1/2	cup honey mustard or Dijon
1	(6 ounce) jar walnut ice cream topping

Place Brie on microwave-safe plate.
Spread with mustard and walnut topping.
Microwave on high 1 1/2 to 2 minutes.
Check every 30 seconds until cheese is soft and just beginning to split.
Serve with crackers.

Serves 20

Sheila Glasser

11

Smoked Bluefish or Smoked Trout Pâté

This entire dish can be put together in minutes, so it's perfect for last minute entertaining.

1/2	cup cream cheese, room temperature
4	tablespoons butter
1/4	cup heavy cream
1	tablespoon horseradish
1/2	teaspoon Tabasco sauce
1	tablespoon lemon juice
1	pound smoked bluefish, filleted, skin removed
	Parsley (garnish)

Beat together all ingredients except fish, until smooth.
Gently beat in smoked fish, refrigerate until serving.
Garnish with parsley.
Serve with crackers or mixed vegetables.

Serves 10

Compliments of Benkovitz Seafoods

Seven Layer Egg and Caviar Dazzler

The blend of these ingredients add a vibrant accent of color when served on little toasts as an hors d'oeuvre. The bold flavors of the bright red caviar and the green onions add just the right touch of pizzazz!

2	(14 1/2 ounce) cans artichoke hearts, drained, chopped
4	hard-boiled eggs, chopped
1	bunch green onions, chopped
1	(5 1/2 ounce) can black olives, drained, chopped
1	(3 1/2 ounce) jar red caviar
	Mayonnaise (spread on top of each layer)
	Paprika (sprinkled on top of each layer)

In a 1 1/2 quart glass bowl, layer half of each ingredient in order given.
Repeat, cover, refrigerate overnight. Serve with party rye and toasts.

Serves 8

Sheila Glasser

Terrific Tantalizing Tuna Mousse

This is light, pretty, refreshing, and one of those foods to enjoy time after time.

2	envelopes unflavored gelatin
1	(10 ounce) can tomato soup
1	(8 ounce) package cream cheese, softened
2	(12 ounce) cans tuna, drained (or salmon)
1	cup mayonnaise
1	onion, grated
1	tablespoon lemon juice
1/8	teaspoon Tabasco sauce
1/2	cup chopped celery

Mix gelatin into undiluted heated soup.
Heat just to boiling and cool.
Place remaining ingredients in mixer or blender.
Add to soup mixture.
Pour into a large fish mold which has been greased with mayonnaise.

Chill for several hours or overnight. Unmold on large platter.
Serve with party rye.

Serves 10

Sally Samuels

Layered Goat Cheese and Pesto

Wonderful with a glass of wine before an elegant meal.

1	cup spinach, coarsely chopped, loosely packed
1	cup fresh basil, loosely packed
1	teaspoon minced garlic
1/4	cup olive oil
1	cup fresh grated Parmesan cheese
	Salt and pepper to taste
1	(8 ounce) package cream cheese, softened
1	(4 ounce) package goat cheese, softened
1/4	cup finely chopped walnuts
1/4	cup sun-dried tomatoes in oil, drained, thinly sliced

Line a 3 cup bowl with plastic wrap, leave a 4-inch overhang.
Combine spinach, basil and garlic in processor.
Chop fine. With machine on, add oil slowly.
Add Parmesan cheese, process until smooth, season with salt and pepper.

Stir cheeses together in medium bowl until blended and smooth.
Spread 1/3 cheese mixture in bottom of prepared bowl.
Spread 1/2 the pesto over cheese.
Top with half of the walnuts, half of the tomatoes.
Repeat layering in this order, spinach, walnuts, tomatoes, end with cheese.
Fold plastic wrap over top, press to compact.
Refrigerate overnight, up to 3 days.

Unwrap, invert onto plate.
Let stand at room temperature 30 minutes.
Serve with crackers.

Serves 6

Sheila Glasser

Lox Cheese Cake Appetizer

Here is a spectacular treatment when simple lox and cream cheese doesn't seem festive enough.

1/2	cup fine bread crumbs
1/2	onion, finely chopped
1/2	green pepper, finely chopped
2	tablespoons margarine
3	(8 ounce) packages cream cheese, softened
4	eggs, beaten
1/3	cup cream
8	ounces ground lox
1/2	cup grated Gruyère cheese

Butter inside of springform pan. Sprinkle with bread crumbs. Chill.
Sauté onion and green pepper in margarine. Combine with remaining ingredients.

Pour into springform pan. Place on sheet of foil and wrap sides.
Bake in 300 degree oven 40 minutes.

Turn off heat, cool 1 hour in oven with door ajar.
Remove, cool completely on rack outside of oven.
Refrigerate before removing sides.
Serve in slices with crackers.

Serves 10 to 12

Cindy Speck

Grandma Ruth's Romanian Style Chopped Eggplant

Cooking, smelling and tasting this smoky flavored dish transports me to my grandparent's house on a Sunday afternoon.

1	**large eggplant**
1 1/2	**tablespoons olive oil**
	Salt and pepper to taste
1	**small onion, chopped (optional)**
1	**celery stalk, minced**
1	**green or red pepper, minced**
1	**tomato, sliced**

Grill or broil eggplant on all sides until tender and almost collapsed.
Cool, slit eggplant, scoop out pulp. Drain eggplant in colander. Chop or mash with a fork.

Add olive oil, salt and pepper to taste. Combine with chopped vegetables.
Serve chilled or at room temperature.
Serve with sliced tomatoes, pumpernickel or rye bread.

Serves 6

Nancy Neudorf

Old-Fashioned Chopped Herring

This appetizer is traditionally served at the 'break the fast' meal following Yom Kippur. Glass containers are best for storage as they do not retain herring odors after cleansing.

1	**(16 ounce) jar herring fillets in wine sauce**
2	**slices day old challah**
2	**hard-boiled eggs**
1	**small apple, peeled and cored**
1	**small onion, quartered**

Drain and save liquid from herring, soak challah in liquid.
Put herring, eggs, apple and onion into a blender or food processor.
Squeeze liquid from bread, add to the rest of ingredients, chop fine.
Refrigerate.
Serve with party rye or crackers.

Yields 2 1/2 cups

Thea Bernstein

Mock Chopped Liver

You will have to prepare this and see for yourself how this 'liver' is a vegetarian's delight.

5	onions, chopped
4	tablespoons oil
10	hard-boiled eggs (use whites only)
1	cup ground walnuts
1	(15 ounce) can tiny peas, drained
2	stalks celery, diced
	Salt and pepper to taste
1	grated hard-boiled egg (garnish)
	Olives (garnish)

Sauté onions in oil, 15 to 20 minutes until caramelized, drain. Reserve oil.
Combine all ingredients in processor for 30 seconds or chop by hand,
(except grated egg).
Peas should be chopped completely.
Add desired amount of reserved oil and salt and pepper to taste.

Grease round ring mold with remaining sauté oil.
Add all ingredients; refrigerate 2 hours.
Unmold, garnish with grated egg.
Fill center of mold with olives. Serve with crackers.

Note: To hasten cooking, microwave chopped onions 5 to 6 minutes to soften.

Serves 6 to 8

Rozalyn Wein

Spicy Dip

Almost everything tastes better with a little dab of this spicy dip on it. Try it with assorted crisp vegetables, tortilla or potato chips.

1	cup mayonnaise
2	tablespoons grated onion
2	teaspoons tarragon vinegar
2	teaspoons chopped chives
2	teaspoons chili sauce
1/2	teaspoon curry
1/2	teaspoon salt
1/8	teaspoon ground thyme

Mix all ingredients together.
Refrigerate until served.

Yields 1 cup

Lea Davidson

Tofu and Cauliflower Dip

This tasty preparation may be served as a dip, salad, or spread on crackers.

1	pound firm tofu, drained
1	cup minced celery
1/2	teaspoon turmeric
4	tablespoon low calorie mayonnaise
1/2	cup minced scallions
1/4	teaspoon salt
1/2	teaspoon low sodium soy sauce
2	tablespoons mustard
1/4	teaspoon black pepper
3/4	cup cauliflower, small florets, steamed crisp
1/8	teaspoon cayenne

Mash tofu until smooth.
Mix all ingredients together.

Serves 15

Marianne Silberman

Gloria's Spicy Glazed Pecans

The cayenne pepper gives these delightful nuts some extra zip. If you make more, you can put them in a bottle, tie a ribbon around it, and give it as a hostess gift.

1/2	**cup sugar**
3	**tablespoons water**
3/4	**teaspoon salt**
1/2	**teaspoon cayenne pepper (or to taste)**
2	**cups pecan halves**

Butter large baking sheet.
Combine first 4 ingredients in small saucepan.
Stir over medium heat until sugar dissolves, about 2 minutes.
Add pecans and stir until nuts are coated.
Transfer nuts to prepared sheet, spreading them evenly.

Bake in 350 degree oven until nuts just begin to brown, about 8 to 12 minutes.
Transfer to cookie sheet lined with waxed paper and separate with fork.
Cool completely. Store in air tight container.

Note: Oven temperatures may differ, check often to prevent burning.

Yields 2 cups

Gloria Janovitz

Hint:
Hors d'oeuvres: when serving hors d'oeuvres on a silver tray, you may wish to protect it from acids by covering it with a layer of leafy green lettuce.

Portobello Mushrooms
with Rosemary-Lime Marinade

The extra virgin olive oil, rosemary, garlic and lime accented marinade offers a hint of sophistication and flavor to these meaty mushrooms.

1	**pound Portobello mushrooms, thickly sliced**
5	**tablespoons extra virgin olive oil**
1	**tablespoon chopped fresh parsley**
1	**sprig fresh rosemary, chopped**
1	**small shallot, chopped**
1	**clove garlic, minced**
	Juice of 2 limes
	Salt and fresh ground white pepper to taste

Combine all ingredients for marinade.
Place mushrooms and marinade mixture in self sealing bag.
Marinate 1 hour. Grill over heat until soft.
Serve warm or room temperature on fresh French bread rounds.

Note: May coat with olive oil, salt and pepper. Grill first, then marinate. Serve chilled.

Serves 2 to 3

Roberta Moore

Hint:

Onions: once an onion has been cut in half, rub the leftover side with margarine and it will keep fresh longer.

Phyllo Champignon

A powerhouse dish that combines the soft texture of eggplant, mushrooms, onions and cheese with the crunch of phyllo.

1	**medium eggplant, cubed**
1	**medium onion, chopped**
1/4	**pound mushrooms, sliced**
1	**clove garlic, crushed**
2	**tablespoons butter**
1 1/2	**cups grated Swiss or jack cheese**
1/2	**cup Parmesan cheese**
2	**eggs, beaten**
1/4	**cup chopped parsley**
1/2	**teaspoon basil**
1/2	**teaspoon oregano**
1	**teaspoon salt**
1	**(1 pound) package phyllo pastry dough**
1	**cup bread crumbs**
1/2	**cup butter, melted**

Sauté eggplant, onion, mushrooms and garlic in butter until soft and brown.
Add all other ingredients except bread crumbs, butter and phyllo.

Place two well buttered pieces of phyllo on flat surface.
Spoon a generous portion of mixture along end of dough.
Sprinkle bread crumbs along remaining surface of phyllo.

Roll up jelly roll fashion.
Place on well buttered cookie sheet.
Bake in 350 degree oven about 10 to 15 minutes until golden brown.
Slice and serve.

Serves 8

Compliments of Lila Grushka Catering
Tucson, Arizona

Boursin Phyllo Tart

This is a very rich appetizer, so make sure that you cut it into small slices. I like to serve it slightly warm. The tantalizing taste of crisp phyllo and velvety Boursin cheese make this delicious tart hard to pass up.

1	**(5 ounce) container Boursin cheese**
1/2	**cup ricotta cheese**
1	**egg, lightly beaten**
1	**tablespoon chopped Italian parsley**
1/4	**teaspoon salt**
5	**tablespoons butter, melted**
6	**sheets phyllo pastry dough**

In a bowl, combine cheeses, egg, parsley and salt.
Brush bottom and sides of an 8-inch loose bottom tart pan with butter.
Brush 1 sheet phyllo with butter, place in pan, allowing excess to overhang pan.

Continue with remaining dough in a circular pattern.
Spread cheese mixture in pan.
Fold over half the phyllo, brush with butter.
Fold over other half, brush again with butter. (This will not look perfect.)

Bake in 375 degree oven 20 minutes or until golden brown.
Remove from oven, cool on rack.
Carefully remove sides of pan and place on serving dish.
Cut into wedges to serve.

Serves 8

Sheila Glasser

Potato Parsnip Pancakes with Smoked Salmon

This is a beautiful dish to behold. Serve this one as the first course of a very elegant dinner.

8	tablespoons crème fraîche (or sour cream)
4	tablespoons prepared white horseradish, (squeeze dry)
2	tablespoons chopped fresh parsley, divided
3/4	pound russet potatoes, peeled
1/2	pound parsnips, peeled
1/2	cup finely chopped onion
3	tablespoons chopped chives, divided
	Salt and pepper to taste
1	large egg, beaten
4	tablespoons olive oil
12	thin slices smoked salmon (about 6 ounces)

Mix crème fraîche, horseradish and 1 tablespoon parsley in a small bowl.
Coarsely grate potatoes and parsnips into medium bowl.
Mix in onion, 2 tablespoons chives and remaining tablespoon parsley.
Season with salt and pepper. Mix in egg.

Divide potato mixture into 4 equal portions.
Heat 1 tablespoon oil in medium nonstick skillet over medium heat.
Add one potato portion to skillet, flatten to a 5-inch round.
Cook until golden brown on bottom.
Turn pancake over, cook until browned and cooked through.
Transfer to oven proof platter , place in 250 degree oven to keep warm.
Repeat with remaining 3 portions, adding 1 tablespoon oil to skillet for each pancake.

Place 1 pancake on each of 4 plates. Arrange 3 salmon slices atop each.
Top each pancake with a dollop of crème fraîche mixture.
Sprinkle with remaining chives, serve immediately.

Serves 4

Compliments of Rania Harris
Rania's Catering

Gravlax

Lovely, impressive, and superbly fragrant, Gravlax is also among the simplest cured dishes. Use king or sockeye salmon when they're in season. This very elegant appetizer can be served with champagne. A great way to toast the New Year.

3-4	**pounds salmon fillet, skinned and boned**
1/3	**cup kosher salt**
1/3	**cup brown sugar**
2	**teaspoons black pepper**
1	**cup fresh dill, chopped**
1/4	**cup mashed green peppercorns with brine**
1 1/2	**tablespoons fresh lemon juice**
1 1/2	**tablespoons brandy**

Garnish: chopped onion, chopped hard-boiled egg, capers

Combine salt, brown sugar and pepper.
Spread mixture evenly over both sides of salmon.
Sprinkle dill and peppercorns on top.
Pour lemon juice and brandy over top.

Fold over and sandwich the fillets together, wrap tightly in plastic.
Press down with a weight, (such as canned goods). Refrigerate three days.

Unwrap fillets, rinse with cold water.
Wrap again in plastic, weight down, refrigerate 7 days longer.
Remove from refrigerator, slice thin on the diagonal.
Serve on rye or pumpernickel bread with garnishes.

Serves 12

Compliments of Café Sam

BREADS AND BRUNCH

BREADS AND BRUNCH

Glazed Lemon Bread

This bread is a fragrant taste-tempting delight.

6	tablespoons butter
3/4	cup sugar
2	eggs
3	tablespoons lemon juice
2	teaspoons fresh lemon zest
1 1/2	cups flour, sifted
1	teaspoon baking powder
1/4	teaspoon salt
1/2	cup milk

Glaze:

3	tablespoons lemon juice
1/2	cup sugar

Cream butter and sugar until fluffy. Beat in eggs, one at a time.
Beat in lemon juice and lemon zest.
Combine flour, baking powder and salt.
To butter mixture, add flour alternately with milk.
Beat just enough to blend.

Line bottom of a greased 8 x 4-inch loaf pan with waxed paper.
Butter paper, pour batter into the pan.
Bake in 350 degree oven 1 hour or until a toothpick inserted in the middle comes out clean.

Blend lemon juice and sugar. Pour slowly over hot bread.
Let bread remain in pan until glaze is absorbed. Cool on a rack.
Remove waxed paper after bread has cooled.

Serves 6 to 8

Charilee Levy

One Bowl Challah

The Challah, or braided egg bread, is the centerpiece of the Shabbat celebration in Jewish homes. The tradition of removing a small piece of dough before baking is symbolic of the contribution of a loaf given to the High Priests in the days of the Temple, as commanded in the Bible.

4	**cups flour**
1	**teaspoon salt**
2-3	**tablespoons sugar**
2	**tablespoons margarine or oil**
1	**egg plus 1 egg white**
1/2	**cup white raisins (optional)**
1	**package dry yeast dissolved in 1/3 cup warm water plus 1 teaspoon sugar (or 1 package fast rise dry yeast)**
1	**cup very hot water**
1	**egg yolk for bread egg wash** **Poppy or sesame seeds (optional)**

Add all ingredients together in order.
For holidays, add raisins to flour mixture before adding yeast.
Mix with hands or mixer with dough hooks until bowl is clean and dough forms a ball.
Flour board, knead until smooth and elastic, 5 to 8 minutes.
Place in greased bowl, cover with towel.
Let rise until double in size (approximately 1 hour and 30 minutes).
(If using fast rising yeast let rise for 50 to 60 minutes.)

Punch down, grease cookie sheet or loaf pans with nonstick spray (see Note).
For a large challah with top braid, cut off 1/3 of the dough and set aside.
Cut remaining dough into 3 parts.
Roll each part into a long strand with hands.
Braid three strands together, place on cookie sheet.
Repeat with dough that was set aside, place smaller braid on top of the larger one.
Let rise 30 minutes for regular yeast, 15 minutes for fast rising yeast.

After dough has risen, mix 1 egg yolk with 4 to 6 drops of water, brush top of challah.
Sprinkle with poppy or sesame seeds or leave plain.
Bake in 350 degree oven 30 to 35 minutes or until golden brown.
Bread should sound hollow when bottom is tapped. Cool on rack.

One Bowl Challah, continued

Note: Before she begins to shape the dough, the traditional woman pinches off a piece of dough the size of an olive and forms it into a ball.
Reciting the following blessing, she tosses this dough into the oven before she bakes the challah:

Baruch atah adonai, elohaynu melech ha-olam, asher kidshenu b'mitzvotov, v'tsivanu l'hafrish challah.
Blessed art though, O Lord our God, King of the Universe, who hath sanctified us by His commandments; and Hath commanded us to separate challah.

Yields 1 large or 2 small challah

Ruth Foreman

Perfect Pumpkin Bread

This is a best seller at any food boutique or volunteer bake sale.

3	cups sugar
1	cup vegetable oil
4	eggs, beaten
1	(16 ounce) can pumpkin
3 1/2	cups flour
1	teaspoon baking powder
2	teaspoons baking soda
2	teaspoons salt
2	tablespoons pumpkin pie spice
2/3	cup water

Cream sugar and oil together.
Add eggs and pumpkin, mix well.
Sift dry ingredients together, add alternately with water.
Pour into 2 well-greased and floured 9 x 5-inch loaf pans.
Bake in 350 degree oven 1 1/2 hours.
Let stand 10 minutes, remove from pans to cool completely.

Yields 2 loaves

Barbara Befferman

Parmesan Cheese Bread

No kneading is necessary for this easy-to-make bread. The wonderful aroma wafting through the house can warm body and soul.

1	**package dry yeast (2 1/4 teaspoons)**
1/4	**cup warm water**
1 1/2	**cups unbleached flour**
1	**tablespoon sugar**
1/2	**teaspoon salt**
1/3	**cup butter**
1	**egg, beaten**
1/4	**cup milk, heated lukewarm or at room temperature**
1/2	**cup grated Parmesan cheese**
1/4	**cup finely chopped parsley**

Dissolve yeast in warm water.
Place flour, sugar and salt in bowl of an electric mixer.
With pastry blender or two knives, cut in butter until mixture resembles coarse meal.
Add egg, yeast and milk.
Beat at low speed 1 minute to blend, add cheese and parsley.
Continue beating at high speed until mixture separates from beaters and soft dough is formed.

(It is not necessary to knead this dough.)
Gather into a ball, place into a greased 8 x 1 1/2-inch round cake pan.
Cover, set in a warm place and allow dough to rise until double in size, about 45 to 60 minutes.

Preheat oven to 350 degrees.
Bake 20 to 25 minutes or until brown, and sounds hollow when tapped.

Yields 1 bread

Compliments of Jane Citron
Food Writer/ Consultant/ Teacher

Philadelphia Whole Wheat Banana Bread

Everyone has a favorite recipe for banana bread. Here's mine.

1/2	cup butter or margarine
1	cup packed brown sugar
2	eggs
1	cup all purpose flour
1	cup whole wheat flour
1/2	teaspoon baking soda
1/2	teaspoon baking powder
1/2	teaspoon ground cinnamon
1	cup mashed bananas
1	cup finely shredded carrots
1/2	cup chopped walnuts

Combine butter or margarine, sugar and eggs.
Mix flours, baking soda, baking powder and cinnamon.
Add dry ingredients alternately with bananas to first mixture.
Fold in carrots and walnuts.
Bake in 350 degree oven 40 to 50 minutes in greased loaf pan.
(If small loaf pans are used, reduce baking time.)

Yields 2 large or 4 small loaves

Iris Steiner

(Submitted by Ruth Foreman)

Hint:
When bread is baking, a small dish of water in the oven will help keep the crust from getting too hard or brown.

Cranberry Pumpkin Muffins

This recipe is one of my favorites as it marries two of my most revered foods, cranberries and pumpkin. It has been a real standby as it virtually never fails no matter if I add additional pumpkin, or use large, medium or small muffin cups.

2	**cups flour**
1	**cup sugar**
1/2	**teaspoon baking powder**
1	**teaspoon baking soda**
1	**teaspoon salt**
1	**teaspoon cinnamon**
1/2	**teaspoon allspice**
1/2	**cup butter, melted**
2	**eggs**
1 2/3	**cups cooked pumpkin, pureed**
1 1/4	**cups fresh cranberries**

Preheat oven to 350 degrees.
Sift flour, sugar, baking powder, baking soda, salt, cinnamon and allspice.
Add butter, eggs and pumpkin.
Mix together with a pastry blender until just combined.
Stir in cranberries.

Fill 18 greased muffin cups almost full (these do not raise much).
Bake 35 minutes or until a toothpick inserted into the center comes out clean.

Yields 18 muffins

Marla Papernick

Hint:
Frozen Bread: put frozen bread loaves in a clean brown paper bag and place for 5 minutes in a 325 degree oven to thaw completely.

Marvelous Moist Zucchini Muffins

Delectable muffins...bet you can't eat just one! These are great with coffee for a morning pick-me-up or afternoon snack.

1	cup salad oil
2	cups sugar
3	eggs, slightly beaten
2	teaspoons vanilla
2	cups unpeeled grated zucchini (do not squeeze)
3	cups flour
1	teaspoon salt
1	teaspoon baking soda
3	teaspoons cinnamon
1/4	teaspoon baking powder
1	cup chopped nuts

Blend together oil, sugar, eggs, vanilla and zucchini.
Stir (do not beat) in flour with other dry ingredients, add nuts.
Fill lined muffin tins 1/2 full. Bake in 375 degree oven 20 minutes.

Yields 24 to 28 muffins

Ruth Zaremberg

Popovers

Nothing is as satisfying as reaching into a basket lined with a colorful napkin, picking up a hot roll, and breaking it open. As the steam pours out, so does the wonderful aroma. Just butter, then bite.

4	eggs
1 1/4	cups milk
1/4	cup butter or margarine, melted
1 1/4	cups sifted flour
1/2	teaspoon salt

Preheat oven to 400 degrees.
Grease muffin tin well.
Beat eggs, add milk and melted butter or margarine, beat.
Add flour and salt to egg mixture, beat until smooth.
Pour evenly into 12 muffin cups.
Bake approximately 25 minutes.

Yields 12 popovers

Dee Selekman

Feather Yeast Rolls

"I've been making this recipe since I worked on a weekly in Gresham, OR., where I met my husband, Ace. He married me for these rolls. They're simple enough for beginners because they don't require kneading, and they're great for Thanksgiving because they can be mixed the night before."

1	**package dry yeast dissolved in 1 tablespoon water**
1 1/2	**cups scalded milk (cooled)**
1/2	**cup sugar**
1	**teaspoon salt**
1/2	**cup butter, melted**
2	**eggs, well beaten**
5	**cups flour**
1/2	**cup additional butter, melted (for brushing)**

Mix all ingredients except flour with an electric mixer.
Stir in flour all at once.
Refrigerate 3 to 4 hours or overnight.

Preheat oven to 350 degrees.
Cut dough into 4 pieces.
Roll 1/4 of dough into circle, brush with melted butter.
Cut circle into 8 pie-shaped wedges.

Roll up from wide to narrow end, tucking under tip; shape into crescent.
Place on nonstick or buttered cookie sheet. Brush with butter.
Repeat with remaining dough.
Let rise 2 hours, or until double in size.
Bake 10 to 12 minutes or until lightly browned.

Yields 32 rolls

Compliments of Suzanne Martinson
Food Editor, Pittsburgh Post-Gazette

Blini with Caviar and Lemon Crème Fraîche

Make a glamorous presentation with this delicate pancake any time of the year.

1/2	cup crème fraîche or sour cream
4	teaspoons minced lemon zest
	Salt and pepper to taste
3/4	cup flour
3/4	cup buttermilk
1/3	cup beaten eggs (about 1 1/2 large eggs)
1/3	cup chopped mixed fresh herbs (parsley, chives, mint, etc.)
2	tablespoons chopped shallots
1 1/2	tablespoons butter, melted
3/4	teaspoon baking powder
1/4	teaspoon baking soda
8	teaspoons butter
4	tablespoons caviar

Blend crème fraîche and lemon zest in a small bowl.
Season to taste with salt and pepper. Set aside.
Mix remaining ingredients together except butter and caviar.

Melt 2 teaspoons butter in a large nonstick skillet over medium heat.
Working in batches, drop batter by heaping tablespoonfuls into skillet.
Spread each blini to 3-inch round with back of spoon.
Add 2 teaspoons butter to skillet for each batch.
Cook until bottom is golden, about 3 minutes.
Turn over, cook until bottom is golden, about 2 minutes.
Transfer to plates.
Top each blini with a dollop of the lemon crème fraîche and caviar.

Serves 12

Compliments of Rania Harris
Rania's Catering

Triple Cheese Blintz Casserole

This is a quick and easy dish to assemble. It's a dairy meal with a difference.

Filling:

1	pound farmer's cheese
1	pound ricotta cheese
1	pound cream cheese
2	eggs
1/2	cup sugar
1/8	teaspoon salt
2	tablespoons lemon juice

Batter:

1	cup margarine, melted
1/2	cup sugar
2	eggs
1	cup flour
1/8	teaspoon salt
3	teaspoons baking powder
1	teaspoon vanilla

Blend together all ingredients for filling.
In another bowl, mix all batter ingredients by hand.
Pour 1/4 of batter into a greased 13 x 9-inch baking dish.
Top with filling and cover with remaining batter.
Bake in 350 degree oven 1 to 1 1/2 hours until golden brown.

Serves 20

Shirley Zionts

Hint:

Greasing pans: use shortening instead of margarine or oil to grease pans, as margarine and oil absorb more readily into dough or batter and do not help to release baked goods from pan (especially bread).

Italian Frittata

This Italian open-faced omelet, filled with tomatoes, cheese and herbs, is cooked on top of the stove and finished off under the broiler. What better proof of how good an egg can be!

	Olive oil
3	**medium onions, thinly sliced**
1	**(14 1/2 ounce) can Italian crushed tomatoes, drained**
6	**eggs**
1	**teaspoon salt**
1/4	**cup grated Parmesan cheese**
	Freshly ground black pepper to taste
2	**tablespoons dried basil**
2	**tablespoons chopped parsley**
2	**tablespoons butter or margarine**

Heat oil in 12-inch skillet. Sauté onions until lightly browned.
Raise heat, add tomatoes, stir 5 minutes. Set aside to cool.

Beat eggs, add salt, cheese, pepper, basil and parsley.
Remove onions and tomatoes from skillet with slotted spoon. Set aside.

Wipe skillet with paper towel, melt butter in skillet (do not brown).
Add eggs, reduce heat to low. Gently put tomato mixture on top of eggs.
Cook until almost done, then brown under broiler.
Cut into wedges and serve immediately.

Serves 4

Ruth Ganz Fargotstein

Mexican Cheese Strata

A Southwestern dish that is prepared the day before. Assemble this on Saturday night and have a delicious brunch dish on Sunday.

4	cups broken tortilla chips
2	cups shredded Monterey Jack cheese
6	eggs, beaten
2 1/2	cups milk
1	(4 ounce) can green chiles, chopped
1/4	cup chopped onion
3	tablespoons ketchup
1/2	teaspoon salt
1/4	teaspoon Tabasco sauce
	Whole tortilla chips and sliced tomatoes (garnish)

Sprinkle broken tortilla chips evenly over a greased 12 x 7-inch baking dish. Sprinkle with cheese.
In a medium mixing bowl, combine remaining ingredients except garnish. Pour over cheese. Cover and refrigerate overnight.

Remove from refrigerator 30 minutes before baking.
Bake in 325 degree oven, uncovered, 50 to 55 minutes until set and lightly browned.
Garnish with tortilla chips and tomato slices.

Note: Egg beaters and low fat milk may be substituted, if desired.

Serves 6

Sharon Dobkin

Grandma Shirley's Thin Pancakes

These pancakes are lighter than air and marvelous served with 'real' maple syrup - a real winner!

1   cup flour
1   egg
1   tablespoon butter or margarine, melted
1   teaspoon salt
1   cup milk (add more if thinner batter is desired)
         Butter or margarine (for frying)
         Pure maple syrup

Mix first 5 ingredients together thoroughly.
In large frying pan, melt enough butter or margarine to cover bottom.
Pour in enough pancake batter to form a circle (pour batter sparingly, these are meant to be thin).

Cook until bottom is golden, 3 minutes.
Flip and cook 2 minutes longer, serve with syrup.

Serves 3

Mickie Diamond

Hint:
Butter: soften butter quickly by grating it.

Mixed Berry French Toast

An attractive alternative to regular French toast that turns breakfast into bliss.

4	cups berries (blueberries, raspberries, blackberries)
1	cup plus 1 tablespoon sugar
1	teaspoon cinnamon
2	large eggs, beaten lightly
1/2	cup milk
1	teaspoon vanilla
10	slices French bread (cut on diagonal, 1/2-inch thick)
	Lightly sweetened sour cream for topping

Preheat oven to 400 degrees.
In a shallow 2 quart casserole, sprinkle berries with 1 cup sugar and cinnamon.
In a bowl, combine eggs, milk, vanilla.
Add bread slices, soak 3 to 5 minutes, turning several times.

Arrange bread single layer over berries, sprinkle with remaining sugar.
Bake in middle of oven 20 to 25 minutes or until bread is golden brown.
Serve topped with a dollop of sour cream.

Serves 6

Marlene Gelman

Soups and Salads

SOUPS AND SALADS

Annie's Vegetarian Vegetable Soup

A colorful garden rainbow packed in a bowl, with all it's various ingredients, this traditional soup is very nutritious.

1/4	cup olive oil
2	onions, chopped
4	celery ribs, sliced
1	(28 ounce) can tomatoes
3	carrots, sliced
1	tube dry vegetable-mushroom soup mix
6	quarts water
1/2	cup barley
1/2	pound mushrooms, sliced
	Salt and pepper to taste
1/4	teaspoon basil
1/4	teaspoon dill
1/4	teaspoon thyme
1	(15 ounce) can corn, drained
1	(16 ounce) package frozen mixed vegetables

In a large soup pot, sauté onions and celery in olive oil until soft.
Add tomatoes, carrots, soup mix and seasoning packet.
Add water, barley and mushrooms, bring to boil, simmer 2 hours.

Add seasonings, corn and frozen vegetables.
Cook 15 minutes longer, adjust seasoning.

Serves 8 to 10

Donna Askin

Fresh Vegetable Basil Soup

The mingling of zucchini, cauliflower, meaty mushrooms and luscious tomatoes are combined all in one mouth watering package.

3	**tablespoons butter or margarine (or nonstick spray)**
1	**medium onion, chopped**
1	**large celery rib, sliced**
3	**large carrots, sliced**
1	**(28 ounce) can tomatoes with juice, diced**
2	**teaspoons pareve chicken bouillon**
2	**cups water**
1	**large potato, peeled, cubed**
1	**teaspoon basil**
1/2	**small cauliflower, florets**
2	**small zucchini, sliced 1/4-inch thick**
1/2	**pound mushrooms, sliced**
1/2	**cup noodles (optional)**
	Salt and pepper to taste
	Parmesan cheese (optional)

In a 5 quart pot, heat margarine. Add onion, celery and carrots.
Cook, stirring occasionally until soft, but not brown.
Combine tomato juice, bouillon and enough water to equal 4 cups.
Add to vegetable mixture. Add potatoes, basil and tomatoes.
Bring to boil, cover, simmer 20 minutes.

Add cauliflower, zucchini and mushrooms. Simmer 10 minutes longer.
Add noodles, simmer until vegetables are tender and noodles soft.
Season with salt and pepper to taste.
Sprinkle Parmesan cheese on top when serving.

Serves 8

Marlene Gelman

Minestrone Al Milanese

This is a meal-in-a-pot soup. It's packed with rice, beans, zucchini and looks really Picassoesque in a bowl! Serve with simple salad and plenty of crusty bread.

1 1/2	pounds dried kidney beans
4	quarts water
3-4	cloves garlic, pressed
1	large onion, chopped
5	tablespoons olive oil
3	large potatoes, unpeeled, large chunks
2	carrots, thickly sliced
5-6	medium zucchini, thickly sliced
1 1/2	cups cut green beans
3-4	medium leeks, sliced
	Salt and pepper to taste
	Parsley, chopped
1	large pinch celery seeds
1-2	teaspoons basil
1	teaspoon oregano
	Large pinch marjoram
1/2	head Savoy cabbage, sliced thin
1/2	cup long-grain rice
6-7	large tomatoes or 1 (28 ounce) can whole tomatoes
1	(6 ounce) can V-8 juice or tomato juice (to thin)

Soak kidney beans overnight in enough water to keep them covered.
Drain and pour into a giant kettle (2 gallons or larger) with 4 quarts water.
Add garlic, onion, and olive oil. Simmer 1 to 1 1/2 hours.

Add potatoes, carrots, zucchini, beans and leeks to pot.
Season with salt and pepper, add all seasonings, simmer 45 minutes longer.

Add cabbage, rice and tomatoes. Simmer 20 minutes, adjust seasoning.
If soup is too thick, thin with V-8 juice or tomato juice and water.
This soup freezes well.

Serves 12 or more

Marlene Silverman

Traditional Gazpacho

Pureed until smooth and then seasoned with a lively tasting mixture of red wine vinegar and olive oil. This cold soup from Spain delights the eye and excites the sophisticated palate.

1/3	cup onion, chopped
2/3	cup green pepper, chopped
1	cup cucumber, peeled, seeded and chopped
3	cups ripe tomatoes, peeled, seeded and chopped
1	clove garlic, peeled and mashed
1	teaspoon salt
	Freshly ground pepper
1	teaspoon paprika
1	tablespoon tomato paste (optional)
3	tablespoons olive oil
3	tablespoons red wine vinegar
1	slice white bread, trimmed of crust
2	cups chicken stock or cold water, divided

Garnish:

1	cup toasted croutons
1	cup snipped green onion tops
1 1/2	cups tomatoes, peeled, seeded and finely chopped
2	tablespoons parsley
1	cup cucumbers, peeled, seeded, chopped and lightly salted

Place 1/2 the vegetables in a food processor or blender.
Blend until smooth.

Mix garlic, salt, pepper, paprika, tomato paste, olive oil and wine vinegar in a small bowl.
Cut bread into small dice, add to dressing, mix well.
When bread has absorbed dressing, add 1/2 to blended vegetables.
Add 1 cup chicken stock, puree until smooth, pour into large bowl.

Process remaining vegetables and broth. Add remaining bread, puree until smooth.
Combine with first batch, adjust seasoning, chill several hours or overnight.

Note: To serve, combine tomatoes with parsley. Arrange garnishes in small bowls and pass at table.

Serves 8

Compliments of Jane Citron
Food Editor/ Consultant/ Teacher

Cream of Carrot Soup

A blend of vegetables that becomes a delectable soup.

1	pound carrots, peeled, sliced
1	pound potatoes, peeled, sliced
2	tablespoons margarine
1/2	cup coarsely chopped onion
6	cups chicken broth (prepared from pareve mix)
1	cup cream
1	cup milk
1/8	teaspoon Tabasco (optional)
1/2	teaspoon Worcestershire (optional)
	Chives, parsley, paprika (garnish)

Melt margarine in 6 quart stock pot.
Add onion and cook briefly while stirring.
Add vegetables and broth.
Bring to a boil, simmer 30 to 40 minutes, until tender.

Pour into blender (or food processor) in small batches, and process until smooth.
Return to pot, add remaining ingredients and bring to a gentle boil.
Garnish with chives, parsley, or paprika.

Note: May serve hot or cold. For pareve, substitute 2 cups nondairy cream, for milk and cream.

Serves 8 to 10

Barbara Befferman

Hint:
Thickener – Instant potatoes are a good thickener for stews.

Egg Lemon Soup with Spinach

This delicious vegetarian soup is thick, lemony and tasty. Equally suitable for a family-style meal or for elegant entertaining and prepared with minimum effort.

2	tablespoons vegetable oil
2	cups finely chopped onions
1	large clove garlic, minced
2	medium carrots, finely chopped
1/2	teaspoon dried dill
5	cups vegetable stock or water, divided
3	eggs
4	tablespoons fresh lemon juice
1	cup brown rice, cooked
1 1/2	cups fresh spinach, stemmed and chopped
1/2	cup garbanzo beans
	Salt and pepper to taste

In a soup pot, sauté onions and garlic in oil until translucent.
Add carrots, dill and 4 cups stock, cover, bring to boil.
Reduce to simmer, cook until carrots are tender, about 10 minutes.

Whisk together eggs, lemon juice and remaining one cup of liquid.
Remove pot from heat, whisk in egg mixture.
Reheat gently, stirring continuously, until egg mixture thickens.
Do not boil or it will curdle.

Stir in rice, spinach and beans, season to taste with salt and pepper.
When soup is hot, serve at once.
The spinach should still be bright green, contrasting nicely with the bits of orange carrot.

Serves 8

Ilene Fingeret

Forest Mushroom Soup

The intense, earthy flavors, fresh and full bodied, is sublime. Serve steaming hot or refreshingly cold - your choice.

1	**pound mushrooms, divided in half**
2	**tablespoons margarine**
1	**cup finely chopped carrots**
1	**cup finely chopped celery**
1	**cup finely chopped onion**
1	**clove garlic, minced**
6	**cups beef broth**
3	**tablespoons tomato paste**
1/4	**teaspoon salt**
	Pepper to taste
	Parsley
1	**bay leaf**
	Sherry (optional)

Chop half of the mushrooms, sauté in margarine.
Add carrots, celery, onion, and garlic, sauté 10 minutes longer.
Add beef broth, tomato paste, salt, pepper, parsley and bay leaf.
Bring to a boil, cover and simmer 1 hour.

Remove bay leaf, blend and strain, if desired.
Slice and sauté remaining mushrooms and add to soup.
May be served hot or cold, with or without sherry.

Serves 6

Marianne Silberman

Hint:
Remove fat from soup: remove fat from soup and stews by adding lettuce leaves to pot. The fat will cling to them. Discard leaves before serving.

Grandma Sara's Split Pea and Lima Bean Soup

This hearty soup and it's abundance of meat, vegetables and noodles is a completely filling meal in a bowl. Perfect for a cold blustery night, this is a hand-me-down from my mother-in-law with love.

5	quarts cold water
3	pounds short ribs and bones
2	cups dried yellow split peas, rinsed
1	(1 pound) package lima beans
4	carrots, cut in 2-inch slices
4	ribs celery, coarsely chopped
2	large onions, chopped
2	cloves garlic, minced
1	tablespoon salt
1	teaspoon fresh pepper
1	teaspoon dried thyme leaves
1/4	teaspoon ground thyme
2	bay leaves
1	teaspoon parsley
1/2	teaspoon marjoram
1/4	teaspoon garlic powder
1/4	teaspoon onion powder
3	chicken bouillon cubes
1	(6 ounce) package wide Halushka noodles

In an 8 quart stockpot, bring water with meat to a boil, skim top.
Cover and simmer 1 hour.
Add split peas, 1/2 of lima beans, 1/2 of all vegetables, all seasonings and chicken cubes.
Cover and simmer 1 hour, stirring often.

Add remaining vegetables and lima beans, cook 30 minutes longer.
Add noodles, season to taste, cook 15 minutes longer or until tender.
Remove meat from bones and return to soup.

Serves 10 to 12

Sheila Glasser

Lentil and Garbanzo Bean Soup

Beans are so versatile, plus they are good for you. We should all eat more beans and less meat, and this soup is a good place to start.

2	tablespoons olive oil
2	large onions, diced
4	medium cloves garlic, diced
3/4	cup lentils
1	(15 ounce) can garbanzo beans (liquid included)
1/2	(6 ounce) can tomato paste
3	cups water
1/2	teaspoon sugar
	Salt and pepper to taste
	Fresh parsley

Brown onion and garlic in olive oil.
Add lentils, garbanzo beans with liquid, tomato paste and water.
Bring to a boil.
Reduce heat, simmer approximately one hour, until soup thickens.
Add sugar, salt and pepper to taste.
Garnish with fresh parsley.

Serves 6 to 8

Ilene Fingeret

Hint:

Lentils: lentils contain no cholesterol and almost no fat. They are high in fiber, carbohydrates, iron and vitamin B. 1 cup dry lentils provides about 3 cups of cooked.

Smooth Pumpkin Soup

This creamy, delicious soup is warm and comforting.

1/2	cup sliced mushrooms
1/2	cup chopped onions
2	tablespoons unsalted margarine or butter
2	tablespoons flour
1	tablespoon curry powder
3	(10 ounce) cans chicken broth
1	(1 pound) can pumpkin
1	tablespoon honey
	Pinch nutmeg
	Salt and pepper to taste
1	(16 ounce) can pareve cream

Sauté mushrooms and onions in margarine until soft.
Sprinkle with flour and curry powder, cook briefly.
Add broth, whisk until smooth, add pumpkin, whisk again.
Add honey, nutmeg, salt and pepper.
Heat thoroughly (do not boil). Add cream right before serving.

Serves 6

Debby Firestone

Squash Soup

The aroma of curry, the smoothness of this beautiful, unusual soup, make it ideal for entertaining.

1/4	cup margarine
2	medium onions, chopped
1	tablespoon curry powder
1	large butternut squash, peeled and chopped
2	apples, peeled and chopped
2	cups water or chicken broth
1	cup apple cider

Sauté onions in margarine and curry powder.
Add squash, apples and water to cover. Cook until tender, about 30 minutes.
Puree the soup in a food processor. Add apple cider and heat through.

Serves 6

Barbara Oleinick

Succulent Fish Chowder

Try this delicately flavored, satisfying soup. The velvety smoothness of cream and potatoes—you won't be disappointed.

4	cups potatoes, diced into 1/2-inch cubes
3	tablespoons diced onions
	Salt and pepper to taste
4	cups stock (fish or vegetable)
1/4	cup flour
1/2	cup butter
5	cups milk, divided
3	pounds scrod, cut into large cubes
3	tablespoons chopped fresh dill
1	tablespoon chopped parsley
1 1/3	cups cream

Place the potatoes, onion, salt and pepper into the stock.
Bring to a boil, simmer 10 minutes, until potatoes are tender.
Make a roux of flour and butter in a large pot.
Cook, stirring constantly 5 minutes.

Add stock mixture, cook 5 minutes, stirring constantly.
Add half of the milk, fish, dill and parsley. Cook 5 to 10 minutes.

Add remaining milk, cream, salt and pepper to taste.
Simmer gently for 5 to 10 minutes (at no time should the soup boil).

Serves 10 to 12

Elaine Beck

Italian Green Been Salad with Mustard Vinaigrette

A bold mix of colors adds to the appeal of this dish. The vivid green of this salad is lovely when served in a glass salad bowl.

2   **pounds green beans, trimmed, ends on**

Mustard Vinaigrette:
3   **tablespoons balsamic vinegar**
1   **tablespoon stone ground mustard**
1   **teaspoon salt**
9   **tablespoons olive oil**

1   **large red onion, halved, thinly sliced**
1   **cup toasted pine nuts, divided in half**
1/2   **cup sun-dried tomatoes, plumped and chopped**
      Salt and fresh pepper to taste
1   **large head radicchio (optional)**
1   **large head Bibb lettuce (optional)**

Cook beans in salted water, about 7 minutes.
Rinse in cold water, drain, pat dry.
Combine vinegar, mustard, salt in medium sized bowl.
Slowly whisk in oil in thin stream.

Combine beans, onions, 1/2 cup pine nuts and tomatoes in large bowl.
Mix in vinaigrette, season with salt and pepper, marinate overnight.
Alternate lettuce leaves over large platter.
Mound beans in center, sprinkle with remaining pine nuts and serve.

Note: May eliminate lettuce, toss ingredients and serve directly from bowl.

Serves 8 to 12

Ilene Fingeret

Marinated Beet and Onion Salad with Feta Cheese

The rosy color of this sweet old-fashioned vegetable deserves a place on modern menus. This salad tastes best if beets have been chilled in dressing for at least 2 hours.

Dressing:

1/4	cup soy sauce
2	tablespoons grainy mustard
1	tablespoon vegetable oil
1/8	teaspoon Tabasco sauce
	Salt and fresh pepper to taste

1	bunch fresh beets
2	tablespoons lemon juice or vinegar
1-2	small red onions, sliced thin
4	ounces feta cheese

Combine ingredients for dressing, set aside.
Cook beets in water and lemon juice 1 hour or until tender.
With gloved hands, remove skins (beets will be very hot).
Cut into odd bite-size chunks, cool.

In a glass bowl, add dressing to beets, refrigerate at least 2 hours.
Just before serving, place thin onion rings on top of beets.
Top with feta cheese and serve.

Note: Beets and dressing may be made 1 or 2 days in advance. Refrigerate separately until ready to use. Canned beets may be substituted.

Serves 4 to 6

Cece Politano

Hint:
Salad: always count on a large handful of greens per person, about 2 cupfuls.

Oriental Cole Slaw

Everyone loves this very different, crunchy and delicious cole slaw. I have my good friend, Annette Barnett, who has a very discriminating palate, to thank for this recipe.

Dressing:

3/4	cup oil (no olive oil)
1/3	cup vinegar
1/2	cup sugar
2	packages seasoning mix from oriental noodles

Salad:

1	(16 ounce) package shredded cole slaw mix
1	cup sunflower seeds, toasted
1	cup sliced almonds, toasted
2	bunches green onions sliced
2	(3 ounce) packages oriental noodles soup, beef flavor

Combine dressing ingredients and mix well.
In large bowl, combine cole slaw, sunflower seeds, almonds and onions.
Pour on dressing and toss until well combined.
Refrigerate 2 hours or overnight.
One hour before serving, crumble 1 1/2 packages of noodles into mixture.
Toss gently and refrigerate.

Serves 10

Sheila Glasser

Hint:

Cold salads: glass plates placed in the freezer before dinner keep salads crisp and chilled as well as display a pretty frosted edge.

Arugula and Escarole Salad
with Blue Cheese, Figs and Warm Port Dressing

Arugula's bold flavor and the crisp texture of escarole team up in this warm salad. The addition of a good port combined with the figs really make this mixture sparkle.

1/3	cup port
1/2	teaspoon sugar
4	ounces dried figs, stems removed (6 large or 12 small)
2	tablespoons balsamic vinegar
3	tablespoons minced shallots (or 1/4 small red onion)
1/4	teaspoon salt
1/4	teaspoon fresh ground pepper
1/4	cup extra virgin olive oil
1	(10 ounce) package mixed baby greens (or 3 cups arugula and 6 cups escarole)
1/4	pound blue cheese, crumbled (preferably Roquefort or Stilton)

Bring port, sugar and figs to boil over high heat.
Cover, reduce heat to low, simmer until soft, (not mushy) 15 minutes.
Reserve liquid in pan, remove figs with slotted spoon.
When cool, quarter and set aside.
Whisk vinegar, shallots, salt and pepper into port. Gradually whisk in oil.

Return figs to dressing, reheat over medium heat.
Stir occasionally, until warm but not steaming.
Toss greens and warm dressing to coat in large bowl.
Divide among 6 serving plates. Sprinkle with blue cheese, serve immediately.

Serves 6

Roberta Moore

Persian Fresh Fruit Salad

Quantities of ingredients are not important. Juices blend together and create a tasty fruit salad.

2-3   seedless oranges, sectioned, with juice
2   cups dates, pitted, chopped
1   cup dried apricots, chopped
    Honeydew and/or cantaloupe, cut into small pieces or balls
    Strawberries, sliced thin
    Kiwi, sliced thin
    Plums, sliced thin (if very sweet)
    Peaches, cut into thin slices (if ripe and sweet)
    Bananas (garnish)

Combine all ingredients at least 3 to 4 hours before serving.
When ready to serve, spoon into individual dessert bowls.
Top with thin slices of banana.

Yield varies

Harriet Kruman

Couscous Salad with Fresh Mint

The textures of this salad are perfectly balanced, and the tastes so complementary.

1 1/4   cups medium couscous
1 1/4   cups cold water
1   green or red bell pepper, diced
3   medium tomatoes, peeled and diced
10   scallions, cut into thirds
    Salt and pepper to taste
3   tablespoons fresh lemon juice
5-8   tablespoons extra virgin olive oil
2   sprigs fresh mint, chopped
1/2   cup flat leaf parsley, chopped

Put couscous in bowl, cover with cold water, stir.
Let stand at least 30 minutes, until tender.
Stir in remaining ingredients and refrigerate.

Serves 6 to 8

Compliments of Harold Caplan
Beth Shalom Caterer

Portobello Mushroom and Pear Salad with Parmesan Dressing

All the ingredients of this terrific salad compliment each other. The attractive colors and textures make this very appealing.

Parmesan Dressing:

1	clove garlic
1/2	tablespoon fresh ginger
2	tablespoons grated Parmesan cheese
1	tablespoon dry mustard
1 1/2	tablespoons honey
1/2	teaspoon salt
1/4	teaspoon freshly ground pepper
1/4	cup tarragon vinegar
1	tablespoon lemon juice
1/2	cup olive oil
1/2	cup canola or vegetable oil
2	large portobello mushrooms
	Olive oil
	Garlic salt
8-10	Romaine lettuce leaves, bite size
2	pears, peeled and cored, sliced
4	thin slices red onion
1/4	cup feta cheese, crumbled

Dressing:

Put garlic and ginger in food processor, mince.
Add cheese, mustard, honey, salt, pepper, vinegar and lemon juice.
Process until well mixed. Add the oils all at once, process for 15 seconds.
(Any unused dressing can be refrigerated for 7 to 10 days.)

Gently wash mushrooms. Remove stems, cut the caps into 1/2-inch slices.
Brush with olive oil, sprinkle with garlic salt. Cook 2 minutes on each side.

Place mushrooms and pears on top of lettuce.
Scatter onion slices around mushrooms and pear, and sprinkle with feta.
Add two or three tablespoons of the dressing over the salad.

Serves 4

Helen Kobell

Chicken Salad Niçoise

Traditionally, this Mediterranean salad is made with tuna fish, but chicken provides a delightful alternative.

3	whole boneless and skinless chicken breasts, poached
1	pound red skinned potatoes, cooked just tender, peeled and julienned
1	cup green beans, steamed until just tender
2	medium carrots, julienned
1	large red pepper, julienned
1/2	cup niçoise olives, drained
1	medium red onion, thinly sliced and cut into 1 1/2-inch pieces
1/4	cup capers, drained
3	tablespoons finely chopped fresh basil
	Fresh cracked black pepper to taste

Dressing:

2	cloves of garlic, minced
1	tablespoon Dijon mustard
2	tablespoons finely chopped fresh basil
2/3	cup freshly squeezed lemon juice
1	cup extra virgin olive oil
	Salt and pepper to taste

Garnishes:

	Mixed spring greens
3	hard cooked eggs, quartered
6	Roma tomatoes, quartered
	Fresh basil

Cut chicken into long, thin pieces, place in large bowl.
Add remaining ingredients, toss to combine.

Dressing:

In small bowl, combine garlic, mustard, basil and lemon juice.
Slowly whisk in olive oil until thoroughly combined.
Add salt and pepper to taste.

When ready to serve, use just enough dressing to moisten the salad.
Toss carefully to combine. Taste for seasoning.

Chicken Salad Niçoise, continued

Line a serving platter with mixed spring greens. Mound chicken salad in middle.
Alternate egg and tomato wedges around outside edge on greens.
Garnish with fresh basil leaves, serve extra dressing on the side.

Serves 6

Compliments of Rania Harris
Rania's Catering

Curried Almond Rice Salad

*This can be made in advance and improves in flavor when refrigerated for a
while before serving.*

1	cup long grain rice, cooked
1/2	cup chopped celery
1/4	cup finely chopped green onions
1/4	cup chopped red bell pepper
2	tablespoons slivered almonds, toasted
1/4	cup oil free Italian dressing
2	teaspoons vinegar
1	teaspoon curry powder

Combine first 5 ingredients in a medium bowl.
Combine Italian dressing, vinegar and curry powder.
Add to rice mixture, toss well, cover and chill.

Serves 4

Sheila Cohen

Sesame Orzo Salad

Shredded carrots and raisins make this a beautiful and colorful main dish salad.

Sesame Dressing:

1	teaspoon salt
1	teaspoon pepper
3/4	cup corn oil
1/2	cup sesame oil
1/2	teaspoon grated orange zest
1/2	teaspoon minced garlic
1	teaspoon soy sauce
1	tablespoon sugar
2	tablespoons thinly sliced green onions
1	teaspoon minced fresh ginger
1/4	teaspoon crushed red pepper flakes
2	tablespoons minced fresh parsley

Salad:

1	pound uncooked orzo
1	tablespoon dark sesame oil
	Salt to taste
3	cups shredded carrots
2	cups raisins
1	cup unsalted sunflower seeds or pine nuts, lightly toasted

Combine all dressing ingredients by hand or in food processor, set aside.

Cook orzo 10 minutes in boiling salted water. Refresh under cold water, drain well.
Toss with sesame oil, cool completely.

Combine orzo with dressing and raisins. Add nuts and carrots just before serving.

Serves 8

Debby Firestone

Indonesian Rice Salad

This is pretty to look at and delicious as well. The raisins and nuts give this an exotic taste

1	cup brown rice, uncooked
1/2	cup raisins
2	scallions, chopped
1/4	cup sesame seeds, toasted
1/4	cup cashews, toasted
1/2	cup thinly sliced water chestnuts
1	cup fresh bean sprouts
1	large green or red bell pepper, chopped
1	rib celery, chopped
	Parsley to taste
1/2	cup snow peas (or green peas)
	Mandarin oranges, coconut or pineapple (optional)

Dressing:

6	tablespoons orange juice
1/4	cup oil
1/2	tablespoon sesame oil
2	tablespoons soy sauce
1	tablespoon dry sherry
	Lemon juice, minced garlic, ginger, salt and pepper (to taste)

Cook brown rice in 1 1/3 cups water, (follow package directions) cool. Combine all ingredients, add to rice. Add dressing and season to taste. This recipe can be doubled.

Serves 6 to 8

Marlene Silverman

Jolene's Rice Salad with Capers and Pine Nuts

This is an irresistible way of serving rice. This woodsy salad tastes as fabulous as one would expect.

Dressing:

2	tablespoons lemon juice
2	tablespoons balsamic vinegar
1	tablespoon minced shallots
3/4	teaspoon salt
1/8	teaspoon Tabasco sauce
1/2	cup olive oil

4	cups water
2	cups long grain rice
1 1/2	teaspoons salt
2	bay leaves
2	tablespoons chopped fresh oregano (or 2 teaspoons dried)
1/2	cup pine nuts, toasted
1/3	cup capers, drained
3	tablespoons chopped chives
	Pepper to taste

Whisk together first 5 ingredients, then gradually add olive oil.

Boil water, add rice, salt, bay leaves and stir.
Cover, cook on low heat 20 minutes or until water is absorbed.
Remove bay leaves and stir well.

Transfer rice to large bowl, add dressing and oregano, toss well.
Refrigerate at least 2 hours.
Before serving, mix pine nuts, capers and chives into rice, season with pepper.

Serves 6 to 8

Ruth Fauman-Fichman

FISH

FISH

Blackened Yellowfin Tuna with Fresh Fruit Salsa

Eye-grabbing color and a near magical ability of this salsa help to transform this entrée into gourmet fare.

Salsa:

1	fresh pineapple, diced
1	fresh cantaloupe, diced
1	pint blueberries
1	tablespoon fresh grated ginger
1	(6 ounce) can pineapple juice
2	tablespoons fresh chopped cilantro
1	yellow Holland pepper, minced
1	red Holland pepper, minced

Tuna:

1	pound tuna steaks, 1-inch thick
1/2	cup plus 2 tablespoons blended olive oil (see Note)
1/2	cup red fish magic seasonings
1	teaspoon fresh lemon juice
	Kale or parsley (garnish)
	Lemon slices (garnish)

Combine all salsa ingredients, cover, chill 1 hour.

Combine oil and seasonings, rub over fish, reserve 2 tablespoons oil.
In a cast iron skillet, with ample ventilation, sear both sides of tuna.
Cook 2 minutes on each side, until just medium rare.
(May finish in 350 degree oven after blackened, until cooked.)

Remove fish to serving plate, keep warm.
Add reserved oil and fresh lemon juice to pan, heat.
Drizzle over fish, top with cold salsa
Garnish with kale or parsley and sliced lemons.

Note: Blended oil may be purchased in gourmet stores and is a blend of olive oil, vegetable oil and soy sauce.

Serves 3

Compliments of Chef Peter Lauterbach
Bravo Franco

Grilled Golden Trout with Dill

Grilling produces moist, delicate flavor. Because these fillets are not as firm as steak fish, it requires a little more care in handling to prevent them from falling apart on the grill. The best tool for grilling flat fish is the basket.

4-6	perch or tilapia fillets, (or 3 to 4 boned trout)
1/2	cup canola or olive oil
1/4	cup minced fresh dill or parsley
1/4	cup fresh lemon juice
3	teaspoons garlic, minced
	Salt and pepper to taste
	Lemon wedges

Preheat grill to very hot and spray grids liberally (or use basket).
Rinse fish and pat dry. Brush generously with oil.
Sprinkle with dill or parsley, lemon juice, garlic, salt and pepper.
Grill 3 to 4 minutes on a side. Serve with lemon wedges.

Serves 2

Compliments of Benkovitz Seafoods

Hot Tuna with Cheese and Almonds

Tuna salads are often the main dish and even the entire meal. This hot dish is a delicious, different version of a popular favorite.

2	(6 1/2 ounce) cans tuna, drained
2	cups chopped celery
2	cups croutons
1/2	cup almonds, chopped or slivered
2	teaspoons dried minced onion
1/2	cup shredded Swiss or Cheddar cheese
2	tablespoons lemon juice
1	cup mayonnaise

Mix all ingredients together. Spoon into a 9-inch quiche pan.
Bake in 450 degree oven 10 to 15 minutes.
Serve hot.

Serves 6

Dee Selekman

Scrod Portuguese

A one dish meal with a Mediterranean flair. Serve with dry wine, salad and crusty rolls, for a filling and delicious supper.

12	ounces scrod fillets
2	teaspoons olive oil
1	large onion, sliced (1 cup)
1	large clove garlic, minced
1/2	pound mushrooms, sliced
1	medium-size tomato, peeled, seeded, chopped
3/4	cup chicken broth (or vegetable broth)
	Oregano to taste
	Salt and pepper to taste
1	tablespoon plus 1 teaspoon dry white wine
1	tablespoon chopped fresh parsley
	Medium-size pitted black olives, sliced lengthwise

Heat oil in small skillet. Sauté onions and garlic until tender, about 3 minutes.
Add mushrooms and tomato, cook, stirring constantly until tender.
Add broth, oregano, salt and pepper. Simmer a few minutes, stir in wine.

Arrange fillets in a shallow 3 cup baking dish. Pour vegetable mixture over fish.
Bake in 400 degree oven 20 minutes or until fish flakes easily.
Remove from oven, garnish with parsley and olives.

Serves 2

Marlene Gelman

Hint:
Frying pan: boil vinegar in a brand new frying pan to keep things from sticking to it.

Sea Bass Almandine

A chef's secret recipe that is now yours to enjoy. Prepare just before serving and collect the compliments.

12	medium sea bass fillets, skinless
4	eggs, beaten
1	cup flour
	Salt and white pepper to taste
1-2	cups oil (for frying)
1/2	cup sliced almonds
1/2	cup butter
	Fresh parsley
	Lemon wedges

Season fish with salt and pepper.
Dredge in flour, dust off. Dip in egg, shake off excess.
Cover bottom of frying skillet with 1/8-inch oil, heat thoroughly.
Gently place bass in hot oil.
Sauté until golden brown on both sides, not to exceed 6 minutes.

Remove bass from skillet. Pat excess oil with clean towel.
Place on serving platter, cover with foil to keep warm.
Discard used oil and wipe skillet clean. Repeat until all pieces are cooked.

On low heat, melt butter. Add almonds, stir until golden brown.
Place sea bass on serving plates. Top with equal amounts of browned almonds.
Serve garnished with fresh parsley and lemon wedges.

Note: This recipe is listed on the Moré menu as 'Virginia Spots'

Serves 4

Compliments of Chef Louie Moré
Moré Restaurant

Tilapia with Garlic

When there's citrus juice in a marinade, it is important not to let the fish sit longer than 1 hour because the citrus will 'cook' the fish. This will warm the hearts of garlic lovers everywhere.

1	**pound tilapia fillets**
1/4	**cup plus 1 tablespoon fresh lime juice**
1	**teaspoon olive oil**
1	**tablespoon unsalted butter**
5	**tablespoons garlic, thinly sliced**
3	**tablespoons flour**
4	**tablespoons fresh chopped cilantro or parsley**
	Salt and freshly ground pepper

Place fish in a 2-inch deep glass or enamel-coated dish. Sprinkle with lime juice. Cover with plastic wrap and refrigerate for 1 hour.

Sauté garlic in oil and butter until lightly browned.
Using a slotted spoon remove garlic and set aside.
Remove fish, (reserve lime juice) pat dry with paper towel.
Dust lightly with flour, shaking off excess.
Fry fish 2 to 3 minutes per side, remove to a warming dish.
(Fish should be moist inside, brown and crisp outside.)

Reheat garlic, stir in lime juice, cilantro, salt and pepper.
Heat just until the cilantro begins to wilt.
Pour over the fillets and serve.

Serves 2

Compliments of Benkovitz Seafoods

Tilapia Picatta with Capers

Tilapia is low in fat and has a mild sweet flavor that pleases the palate.

1	**pound tilapia fillets**
4	**tablespoons flour**
4	**tablespoons peanut oil**
1/2	**cup dry white wine**
4	**tablespoons unsalted butter**
1	**teaspoon capers, minced**
2	**tablespoons whole capers**
2	**lemons, juiced**
2	**tablespoons parsley**
	Salt and pepper to taste

Dust fillets with flour.
In heavy ovenproof skillet, over medium heat, brown in oil, 2 minutes per side.
Remove fish and drain excess oil.
Deglaze pan with white wine, add butter, minced and whole capers.

Place fish back into pan.
Bake in 450 degree oven for 5 to 7 minutes, until cooked, place on warm plates.
Add lemon juice, salt and parsley to pan. Mix well, pour over fish and serve.

Serves 2

Compliments of Benkovitz Seafoods

Hint:

Hot oil: to prevent hot oil from splattering, sprinkle a little salt or flour in the pan before frying.

Cold Pickled Salmon

Make this three days ahead and enjoy a different taste that is sure to please any salmon lover.

1 1/2	**cups vinegar**
3/4	**cup water**
1	**teaspoon pickling spices**
2	**large onions, sliced**
1/2	**cup sugar**
1	**whole (3 pound) salmon, cut into 1-inch thick slices**

Place vinegar, water, spices, onions and sugar in large shallow pot.
Bring to boil, simmer 10 minutes.
Put slices of salmon side by side on top of onions.
Cook slowly, 15 minutes, cool.

Refrigerate for at least 3 days before serving.
(Fish must be covered with liquid while in the refrigerator.)
Fish will keep refrigerated for 2 weeks.

Yields 3 pounds salmon

Thea Bernstein

Hint:

Herb butter: make flavored butters by simply combining softened butter with any combination of chopped herbs. Shape into log and refrigerate. Slice onto fish or vegetables.

Dishwasher-Poached Salmon

You will be stunned at the richness of flavor. There is nothing simpler, few things better! A great 'special occasion dish.' Serve hot or chilled with your favorite sauce on the side.

3	**pounds salmon**
1/4	**cup fresh lemon juice**
1	**bunch fresh dill**
	Salt and pepper (optional)

Garnish:

2	**lemons, sliced**
	Fresh dill
1	**cucumber, sliced thin**

Place salmon on heavy duty aluminum foil.
Season with lemon juice, dill, salt and pepper.
Bring up edges of foil, roll and crimp the foil to seal tightly.
Place on top rack of dishwasher. Put through wash and rinse cycle (not dry).

Open dishwasher door, open foil and check for doneness.
If not completely cooked, cover and continue with dry cycle.
When completed, transfer fish to large platter, cool 5 minutes.

Carefully peel off skin, discard cooked dill.
Garnish with lemon slices, fresh dill and cucumbers shortly before serving.

Serves 6

Dee Selekman

Hint:

Grilling fresh herbs: throw whole sprigs onto coals when grilling. The smoke from the burning herbs will flavor whatever is cooking above.

Grilled Salmon with Cucumber Dill Sauce

This combination is a wonderful delight that will surely please the pallet.

Cucumber Dill Sauce (prepare in advance):

1 1/2	tablespoons vegetable oil
1	sweet onion, sliced thin
1	cucumber, peeled, halved, seeded and chopped
1/4	cup white wine vinegar
1 1/2	tablespoons sugar
1	sprig fresh dill, chopped
	Salt to taste

6	(7 ounce) salmon fillets, skin on
	Olive oil
	Salt and pepper to taste

Sauce:

Lightly sauté onion in vegetable oil.

Add cucumber, vinegar and sugar, simmer 5 minutes.

Add dill and salt to taste, cool. Serve at room temperature.

Salmon:

Brush salmon with olive oil, salt and pepper. Grill, skin side up, 4 to 5 minutes. Turn over, cook until center is light pink. Remove from grill with spatula. Serve with cucumber dill sauce on side.

Note: Skin retains the moisture and flavor of fish while cooking, and will burn off.

Serves 6

Compliments of Chef David Conley

Poli Restaurant

Herb-Grilled Salmon with Mango Salsa

Exotic, rich, and totally refreshing, this salsa takes about 20 minutes to make and is best made ahead and refrigerated.

Mango Salsa:

1	cup cubed mango
1	cup sliced banana
1/4	cup fresh mint, chopped
2	tablespoons fresh orange juice
1	tablespoon fresh lime juice
1	(8 ounce) can pineapple chunks, drained
1	serrano chile, seeded

4	(6 ounce) salmon fillets
1/4	cup fresh cilantro, chopped
1/4	cup fresh mint, chopped
1	teaspoon hot pepper oil

1/2	teaspoon salt
1/4	teaspoon pepper
	Rice

Salsa (make in advance):
Combine all salsa ingredients in a medium bowl, stir and refrigerate.

Salmon:
Combine first 4 ingredients in a large zip top plastic bag, shake gently to coat. Marinate in refrigerator 20 minutes. Remove, sprinkle with salt and pepper.

Place on grill or broiler pan coated with nonstick spray.
Cook 5 minutes on each side or until salmon is done.
Serve with mango salsa and rice.

Note: Salsa keeps fresh only about 24 hours.

Serves 4

Marianne Silberman

Homemade Salmon Burgers

A new twist to a classic favorite recipe of ours and is sure to be one of yours.

1	**(6 ounce) salmon steak or fillet**
4	**scallions, sliced, divided**
1/3	**cup plain bread crumbs**
2	**tablespoons tomato puree or ketchup**
1	**egg white**
	Salt and pepper to taste
1/3	**cup nonfat mayonnaise**
2	**tablespoons fresh chopped dill or 2 teaspoons dried**
2	**bread rolls**
1	**small tomato sliced**

Remove fat, skin or dark meat from the salmon.
Cut into 2-inch cubes, chop in food processor.
Add 2 sliced scallions, bread crumbs, tomato puree and egg white.
Add salt and pepper, combine well.

Form into 2 patties about 1/2-inch thick.
Heat a nonstick skillet and brown patties on one side.
Lower heat slightly, cook 3 minutes, turn, cook 2 minutes more.

Mix mayonnaise, remaining scallions and dill together, season to taste.

To serve, place salmon patty on a roll, top with mayonnaise and tomatoes.
Patties freeze well.

Serves 2

Jessy Stein

Maple Glazed Grilled Salmon with Fruit Salsa

This is the kind of dish you'd pay a small fortune for in a restaurant, yet it's quite simple and very impressive

Salsa:

1/2	cup diced cantaloupe
1/2	cup fresh diced pineapple
1/2	cup diced mango
1/4	cup diced red bell pepper
1/4	cup diced yellow bell pepper
1/4	cup diced red onion
2	tablespoons fresh squeezed lime juice
2	tablespoons brown sugar
2	tablespoons minced fresh mint leaves
1	teaspoon minced jalapeño pepper
	Salt and pepper to taste
1/2	teaspoon minced lime zest
4	(6 ounce) salmon fillets
1	cup maple syrup
2	tablespoons cracked mixed peppercorns

Salsa:

Combine all salsa ingredients together in medium bowl.
Cover and chill while grilling salmon.

Salmon:

Combine maple syrup and peppercorns.
Dip salmon into maple glaze just before grilling.
Heat grill to a medium high temperature.
Grill salmon about 4 minutes per side. Do not overcook.
While salmon is cooking, heat remaining glaze to a boil.

To Serve:

Place salmon on center of serving plate, spoon salsa around salmon.
Drizzle small amount of glaze over grilled salmon.

Serves 4

Compliments of Rania Harris
Rania's Catering

Oven Steamed Salmon and Fresh Vegetables

A medley of ingredients producing perfect harmony

4	salmon steaks, 3/4-inch thick (or 1 1/4 pound salmon fillets)
3	tablespoons fresh lemon juice, divided
1	pound small unpeeled new potatoes, quartered
4	medium carrots, peeled sliced in half
2	medium leeks, sliced 1/4-inch thick
1	medium onion (or 6 pearl onions), diced 1/2-inch thick
3	ounces shallots, halved
3	tablespoons lite olive oil
	Salt and pepper to taste
2	small zucchini, sliced 1/4-inch thick
1/2	pound mushrooms, sliced 1/2-inch thick
1	red pepper, sliced
4	tablespoons fresh chives

Preheat oven to 400 degrees.

Sprinkle fish with 2 tablespoons lemon juice, set aside.

Combine potatoes, carrots, onions, leeks and shallots in 9 x 13-inch baking dish.

Drizzle with olive oil, salt and pepper, stir.

Bake 30 minutes until potatoes are tender, stirring twice.

Stir zucchini, mushrooms and peppers into vegetables.

Bake 10 minutes, remove from oven (retain oven temperature).

Add 1 tablespoon lemon juice and 1 tablespoon chives to vegetables.

Arrange fish in pan pushing vegetables to side, spooning leeks, onions, and shallots over fish. Sprinkle chopped chives over all.

Bake 10 to 15 minutes. Do not over cook.

Note: May par-cook potatoes in microwave 4 to 5 minutes before adding to casserole.

Serves 4

Florie Krell

Salmon Mousseline with
Artichoke and Roasted Pepper Beurre Blanc

This delicious mousseline topping, loaded with calories, will turn a plain piece of salmon into a superb dish. The addition of artichokes and roasted red peppers, seasoned with white wine and cream, will make the finest sauce.

Mousseline:

8	ounce salmon fillets, skinned
2	eggs
2	cups heavy whipping cream
	Salt and pepper to taste

Sauce:

1	teaspoon minced shallots
1/4	cup white wine
1/4	cup heavy cream
1	cup butter, cubed
2	tablespoons minced roasted red peppers
2	tablespoons diced artichokes
	Salt and pepper to taste
4	(6 ounce) salmon fillets, skin removed

Mousseline:

Puree 8 ounces of salmon in food processor, add eggs, blend well.
Add cream slowly, blend until light and airy, add salt and pepper to taste.

Sauce:

Boil shallots and wine in sauce pan, reduce to 2 tablespoons.
Add cream, cook until reduced to a glaze, 3 to 5 minutes.
Remove from heat, whisk in butter one piece at a time.
Stir until smooth, add peppers, artichokes, salt and pepper to taste.

Salmon:

Top each (6 ounce) fillet equally with pureed salmon mixture.
Bake in a 375 degree oven for 15 to 20 minutes until cooked and golden brown.
Spoon sauce over salmon and serve.

Serves 4

Compliments of Chef Mark Castelli
Asiago

POULTRY

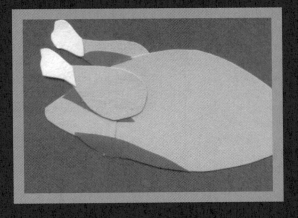

POULTRY

265 Calorie Meal

Who's counting calories these days? Almost all of us are. This recipe gets help from reduced-calorie products while keeping all the flavor.

1	**pound chicken breasts, boneless, skinless, quartered**
1	**(2 1/2 ounce) jar sliced mushrooms, drained**
1 1/2	**cups light Italian dressing**
1/4	**cup chopped onion**
1	**tablespoon margarine**
2	**cups sliced zucchini**
1	**large firm tomato, cut into wedges or 1 (8 ounce) can tomatoes**
1/4	**cup white wine (optional)**
2	**tablespoons flour**
1/8	**cup water**
	Rice

In shallow baking dish, cover chicken and mushrooms with Italian dressing. Marinate 30 minutes, drain, reserve marinade.

In large skillet, cook onion in margarine until tender. Add chicken and mushrooms.
Cook, covered over medium heat until chicken is tender.

Add zucchini, tomatoes, wine and reserved marinade.
Cook and stir until zucchini is tender.
(Combine flour and water, use to thicken sauce, if desired.)
Remove from heat. Cover and let stand for 2 minutes.
Serve with rice.

Serves 4

Florie Krell

Bistro Braised Chicken with Cilantro Tomato Sauce

This chicken is swathed in luxurious cilantro, the smoothness of wine and the mellowing bite of garlic, all to give it a southwest tang. A food processor makes this a simple thing to do.

2	pounds chicken breasts, skinless, boneless
	Flour (seasoned with salt and pepper)
3	tablespoons margarine
3	tablespoons olive oil
1/2	cup cilantro, chopped
1	large clove garlic
1	(14 ounce) can whole peeled tomatoes
2	tablespoons lemon juice
1/4	cup wine or vermouth
	Red onion strips
	Noodles or rice

Dust chicken with seasoned flour, sauté in margarine and olive oil.
When browned on both sides, remove to a warmed plate.

In food processor, mix cilantro, garlic and tomatoes until chunky.
In frying pan, add lemon juice and wine, boil to reduce, about 5 minutes.
Add tomato sauce and chicken to pan, simmer 5 to 6 minutes.
Remove to serving platter and garnish with red onion strips.
Serve over noodles or rice.

Serves 4

Ruth Fauman-Fichman

Hint:

Garlic: peel garlic and store in a covered jar of vegetable oil. The garlic will stay fresh and the oil will be nicely flavored for salad dressings.

Cashew Chicken Stir-Fry with Broccoli and Peppers

This Cantonese recipe is a very simple home-style stir-fry and you will be delighted at how easy it is to impress your friends.

1	pound chicken breasts, skinless, boneless, cut into 1-inch cubes
1	tablespoon cornstarch
2	teaspoons vegetable oil
1	large green pepper, sliced
2	cups frozen broccoli
1	(10 ounce) can baby corn
1	teaspoon minced garlic

Sauce:

1/3	cup soy sauce
1/3	cup orange juice
1/3	cup water
1	tablespoon cornstarch
1	teaspoon sesame oil
	Cashews (garnish)

Shake chicken in bag with cornstarch.
Stir-fry in large skillet 3 to 5 minutes, remove, keep warm.

Add peppers to skillet, stir-fry over high heat 1 minute.
Add broccoli, corn and garlic, cook for 2 minutes.
Combine sauce ingredients, add to skillet, bring to a boil.
Reduce heat, simmer, stir until tender and sauce is slightly thickened.
Return chicken to skillet, heat and sprinkle with cashews.

Serves 4

Marianne Silberman

Arroz Con Pollo (Chicken and Yellow Rice)

This dish is one of glories of Cuban gastronomy. It is made with short-grain Valencia-style rice. Alternatively, you can use any regular rice from the supermarket.

1	**teaspoon dried oregano**
1	**teaspoon ground cumin**
2	**tablespoons lemon juice**
	Salt and pepper to taste
1	**(4 pound) chicken, cut into 8 pieces**
2	**tablespoons olive oil**
2	**medium onions, finely chopped**
1	**green bell pepper, diced**
3	**cloves garlic, minced**
1	**small tomato, seeded and diced**
1	**chicken bouillon cube**
1	**can beer**
3	**cups water**
1/2	**teaspoon saffron**
1	**tablespoon tomato paste**
1/4	**cup pimento stuffed green olives**
	Salt and pepper to taste
2	**cups rice**
1	**cup frozen sugarless tiny peas, divided**
1/2	**cup red pimentos, drained, diced (divided)**

Mix first 5 ingredients in large glass bowl.
Marinate chicken at least 30 minutes, or overnight.

Heat oil in a large frying pan, brown chicken over medium-high heat.
Remove chicken, pour out all but 2 tablespoons of oil.
Add onion, green pepper and garlic.
Cook until soft, add tomato, cook 1 minute.
Combine chicken cube, beer and enough water to make 4 cups.
Add 1 cup of liquid, saffron, tomato paste, olives, salt and pepper to pan, boil.

Reduce heat, return chicken to pan, simmer 30 minutes.
Stir in rice and remaining liquid.
Cover, simmer until rice is tender, 20 to 25 minutes. (Add water if too dry.)

Arroz Con Pollo (Chicken and Yellow Rice), continued

(If mixture looks soupy, remove cover during last 5 minutes of cooking.)
Just before rice is finished, stir in half of the peas and pimentos.
Use remaining peas and pimentos to garnish top, serve at once.

Serves 6

Dorita Krifcher

Balsamic Chicken

This is one dish that always gets accolades. Prepare ahead and refrigerate overnight for added depth of flavor.

1/3	cup vegetable oil
1/2	cup balsamic vinegar
3	tablespoons sugar
3	tablespoons ketchup
1	tablespoon Worcestershire sauce
2	medium scallions, minced
1	teaspoon salt
1/2	teaspoon cracked black pepper
1	teaspoon dry mustard
1	medium clove garlic, minced
5	pounds chicken, cut up

Combine all ingredients and pour over chicken, coat thoroughly.
Marinate in refrigerator 8 hours or overnight, turn occasionally.
Bake in 325 degree oven 60 minutes or until tender.

Note: Chicken may be baked in a 325 degree oven for 30 minutes and then grilled for 4 to 5 minutes per side. Baste often with marinade while grilling.

Serves 4 to 6

Sharon Bodkin

Chicken Breasts On a Bed of Carrots and Mushrooms

The rich flavor of mushrooms and carrots combined with vermouth turns this into a very special course.

1/2	cup water
1	teaspoon lemon juice
6	tablespoons margarine, divided
2	cups sliced mushrooms
2	pounds carrots, julienned
2	tablespoons chopped shallots
1	tablespoon flour
1 1/2	cups chicken broth
8	chicken breast halves, boneless, skinless
1	tablespoon chopped tarragon
	Salt to taste
	Freshly ground pepper to taste
1/4	cup dry vermouth
2	tablespoons chopped parsley (garnish)

Bring water, 1/2 teaspoon lemon juice and 1 tablespoon margarine to a boil.
Add mushrooms, cover, cook 2 to 3 minutes, drain and set aside.

Heat remaining 5 tablespoons margarine in large sauté pan.
Add carrots and shallots, sauté 5 minutes.
Sprinkle in flour, stir constantly for 2 minutes until slightly cooked.
Stir in broth, place chicken pieces on top of carrots.
Sprinkle with tarragon, salt and pepper to taste.
Cover and simmer 10 to 15 minutes.

With slotted spoon, remove chicken and carrots to a warm plate.
Add vermouth and 1/2 teaspoon lemon juice to the pan liquids.
Cook rapidly to reduce slightly, adjust seasonings.
Return chicken, carrots and mushrooms to pan.
Add the parsley before serving.

Serves 4 to 6

Susan Leff

Chicken Ratatouille

In this Moroccan version of a vegetable stew, the chicken soaks up all of the wonderful flavors of the ratatouille.

1/4	cup oil
2	whole chicken breasts, boneless, skinless, 1-inch cubes
1	clove garlic, chopped
2	small zucchini, unpeeled, sliced
1	small eggplant, peeled, 1-inch cubes
1	large onion, thinly sliced
1	medium green pepper, sliced thin
1/2	pound mushrooms, sliced
1	(6 ounce) can tomatoes
2	teaspoons garlic salt
1	teaspoon dried basil, crushed
1	teaspoon dried parsley
1/2	teaspoon black pepper
	Rice

Heat oil in large pan, sauté chicken 2 minutes on each side.
Add next 6 ingredients.
Cook, stirring occasionally 15 minutes, until crisp tender.

Add tomatoes, seasonings and herbs, stir carefully.
Simmer 5 minutes.
Serve on large platter with mound of rice in center.

Serves 4

Marlene Gelman

Chicken with Dried Fruit and Almond Stuffing

This chicken is different from any I have ever tasted. The special flavor comes from the sweet, tart taste of the dried fruit, combined with the crunchy almonds. Stuff two chickens, and don't worry about leftovers - it tastes just as good cold or reheated.

5	tablespoons oil, divided
2	onions, coarsely chopped
1/2	cup dried apricots, coarsely chopped
1/2	cup prunes, coarsely chopped
1/2	cup whole almonds, toasted
1/4	cup golden raisins
1/4	teaspoon cinnamon
1	teaspoon dried tarragon
1/2	teaspoon dried thyme
	Salt and freshly ground pepper to taste
1	(6 pound) whole chicken

Preheat oven to 375 degrees.
In large skillet, heat 2 tablespoons oil.
Sauté onions until transparent.
Sprinkle half the onions onto a foil-lined large shallow roasting pan, set aside.
Add remaining ingredients to onions in skillet, except oil and chicken.
Sauté for 5 to 10 minutes, mixing well. Cool.

Stuff chicken with the mixture and truss.
Place chicken, breast side down on onions in baking pan.
(If any stuffing is left over, sprinkle it around the chicken.)
Rub chicken with remaining 3 tablespoons oil.
Roast 30 minutes, until skin is light golden brown.
Turn, continue baking 30 minutes longer, or until well-browned and crisp.
Serve immediately.

Serves 6

Ilene Fingeret

Chicken with Peas and Mushroom Sauce

This tasty, beautiful and simple recipe features some of our favorite flavors - great chicken, peas and mushrooms. It's a mouth-watering combination.

8   chicken breast halves, skinless and boneless
1/2   cup margarine, melted
3/4   cup seasoned bread crumbs
1   cup chicken broth
1/2   cup sherry
1   tablespoon cornstarch
3/4   pound mushrooms, sliced
1   (10 1/2 ounce) package frozen peas

Dip chicken into melted margarine, then in bread crumbs.
Place chicken, single layer, into a greased 9 x 13-inch baking dish.
Bake in 350 degree oven 40 minutes.

In a small saucepan, combine broth and sherry.
Add cornstarch, simmer until thick. Add mushrooms and peas and heat.
Pour gravy over chicken, bake 15 minutes longer.

Serves 4

Shirley Katz

Forty Cloves of Garlic Chicken

You may be surprised at how mild all this garlic becomes. After long cooking, the cloves perfume the chicken and becomes buttery.

4   whole chicken legs and thighs
4   whole chicken breasts
40   cloves garlic, peeled (not crushed)
6   celery stalks, sliced 2-inch pieces
6-8   carrots, sliced 2-inch pieces
2   onions, quartered
1/2   cup white wine or apple juice

Combine chicken, vegetables and juice.
Place in a 6 quart ovenproof casserole or roaster.
Bake covered in 375 degree oven 2 1/2 hours.

Serves 4 to 6

Caren Heller

Chinese Ebony Chicken

A mahogany honey-soy glaze, marinated ahead, makes this a handsome presentation.

Marinade:

1/2	cup soy sauce
1/4	cup lemon juice
2	tablespoons honey
2	teaspoons oriental sesame oil
1	teaspoon dry mustard
1/2	teaspoon ground ginger
1	clove garlic, minced
1/4	teaspoon ground pepper

1	(3 pound) whole chicken

Combine marinade ingredients and mix well. Add chicken.
Cover and refrigerate at least 1 hour or overnight.

Place chicken, breast side down, on rack in roasting pan.
Bake in 350 degree oven 1 1/2 hours, basting every 15 minutes.
Roast until chicken is dark brown and fork tender.
Serve hot or cold.

Serves 4

Roz Sherman

Hint:

Dry mustard: taste dry mustard for sharpness. You may need to increase the amount if it's been on the shelf a long time.

Drunken Chicken

Quick and company quality. The combination of flavors in this dish is very good, and it makes an impressive presentation.

4	**whole chicken breasts, boneless and skinless**
	Salt and pepper to taste
1	**cup flour**
2	**tablespoons olive oil**
2	**tablespoons margarine**
1	**large onion, minced**
2	**tablespoons minced fresh parsley**
1	**(14 1/2 ounce) can diced tomatoes, undrained**
1/4	**teaspoon ground cloves**
1/2	**teaspoon cinnamon**
1/4	**cup light brown sugar**
1	**cup vermouth**
1/2	**cup golden raisins**
1/2	**cup slivered almonds**

Season chicken with salt and pepper, dust with flour.
Brown chicken in oil and margarine.
Place browned chicken in shallow 8 x 11-inch casserole.

In same skillet, cook onion until transparent.
Add remaining ingredients except almonds.
Simmer, uncovered, 15 to 20 minutes, stirring occasionally.
Pour over chicken and sprinkle with almonds.
Bake in 375 degree oven, 30 to 45 minutes, until tender.

Serves 4

Edy Baron

Grilled Chicken Breasts with Orange Sauce

It is simple to cook with fruit, and fruit also adds color which can turn a predict-able mid-week meal into a festive occasion.

Orange Sauce (make in advance):

2	tablespoons sugar
1/2	cup orange juice
2	tablespoons margarine
2	tablespoons flour
2	ounces Grand Marnier (optional)
2	cups orange marmalade

6	large chicken breast halves, skin on
	Olive oil
	Salt and pepper
1	(11 ounce) can mandarin oranges, drained (garnish)

In a saucepan, dissolve sugar in orange juice.
Over medium heat, cook until juice starts to caramelize in color.
In another saucepan, heat margarine, add flour, stir, add broth.
Add to juice with remaining ingredients, reduce by 1/3.
Remove from heat, cool, set aside. (To reheat, just lightly warm up.)

Brush chicken with olive oil, season with salt and pepper.
Grill chicken turning once or twice until cooked.
Spoon orange sauce over top, garnish with oranges.

Serves 6

Compliments of Chef David Conley
Poli Restaurant

Jamaican Jerk Chicken

A deliciously different dish. Basting with this savory marinade adds flavor and keeps it moist and juicy.

1	tablespoon ground allspice
1	tablespoon dried thyme
1/2	teaspoon cayenne pepper
1 1/2	teaspoons ground black pepper
1 1/2	teaspoons ground sage
3/4	teaspoon nutmeg
3/4	teaspoon cinnamon
2	tablespoons salt
2	tablespoons garlic powder
1	tablespoon sugar
1/4	cup olive oil
1/4	cup soy sauce
3/4	cup white vinegar
1/2	cup orange juice
	Juice of 1 lime
1	cup white onion, chopped
3	scallions, chopped
4	(6 to 8 ounce) chicken breasts

Combine all dry ingredients in a large bowl.
Combine all liquids and onions, slowly whisk together with dry ingredients.
Add chicken to marinade, marinate at least 1 hour or overnight.

Grill chicken or bake in a 350 degree oven until cooked.
Baste often with marinade while cooking.
Boil marinade and serve for dipping sauce.

Note: This is a mild sauce, for spicier flavor, add more cayenne or fresh jalapeños.

Serves 4

Compliments of Chef Victor Tome
Union Grill Restaurant

Javanese Chicken Curry

A great buffet dish which can be made a day ahead. Can be served with green onion rice.

5	**pounds chicken breasts (or 2 cut-up chickens)**
3	**cups water**
3	**teaspoons instant chicken broth**
2	**tablespoons margarine**
1	**large onion, diced**
2	**cloves garlic, minced**
1/4	**cup flour**
1-1 1/2	**tablespoons curry powder**
2	**teaspoons ground coriander**
1 1/2	**teaspoons salt**
1/2	**teaspoon pepper**
1	**tablespoon lemon zest**
2	**tablespoons lemon juice**

Combine water and chicken broth in large saucepan.
Add chicken, cook 30 minutes or until tender.
Remove chicken and measure cooking liquid. Skim off fat.
Return to saucepan, boil until reduced to 3 cups, reserve.
Discard skin from chicken, remove meat from bones, cut into bite size pieces.

Melt margarine in large saucepan.
Sauté onions and garlic until tender, remove from heat.
Combine flour, curry, coriander, salt and pepper.
Sprinkle over onions, stir to coat.

Gradually stir in 3 cups reserved chicken broth until mixture is smooth.
Return to heat.
Bring to boil, reduce heat, cover, simmer 15 minutes, stirring often.
Add lemon zest, lemon juice and stir into curry.
Add chicken, heat thoroughly.

Serves 8

Connie Smolar

Julia's Delicious Chicken and Apricots

The subtle flavor of chicken pairs beautifully with the tender, moist apricots and prunes. Originally, a hand-me-down from my grandmother, I've tinkered with the recipe over the years to come up with this delicious version.

6	chicken breast halves, skinless, boneless
	Salt and pepper to taste
2	cloves garlic, crushed
1/2	cup raisins
1/2	cup dried apricots
1/2	cup dried prunes
1	cup red wine
1/2	cup brown sugar
1/2	cup honey
1	cup water

Preheat oven to 375 degrees.
Season chicken with salt, pepper, garlic.
Combine remaining ingredients, pour over chicken.
Bake uncovered 30 minutes.
Cover, reduce heat to 350 degrees, bake 20 minutes longer or until cooked.

Serves 6

Julia Luovich

Hint:

Garlic cloves can be kept in freezer. When ready to use, peel and chop before thawing.

Oven-Baked Chicken Loaf

A healthy alternative to beef, this chicken entrée will bring lots of 'oohs' and 'aahs' when you serve it.

1	medium onion, minced
2	garlic cloves, minced
1	tablespoon vegetable oil
1 1/2	pounds ground raw chicken breast
1	medium potato, grated
1/2	cup chopped fresh parsley
3	tablespoons ice water
2	tablespoons light soy sauce
	Fresh ground pepper to taste

Sauté onion and garlic in oil until golden.
Combine with chicken and potato, add parsley, mix again.
Add the ice water, soy sauce and pepper to taste. Mix again, gently.
Place into a loaf pan sprayed with nonstick cooking spray.
Bake in 375 degree oven 30 minutes, then broil the top for 3 minutes.

Serves 6

Harriet Kruman

Hint:

Parsley: keep parsley fresh and crisp by storing in a wide-mouth jar with a tight lid. Parsley may also be frozen.

Quick and Easy Chinese Style Chicken

You will be amazed at how authentic this tastes. You may say good-bye to Chinese take-out forever.

Sauce:

1/2	cup plum jam
2	tablespoons orange juice
1	tablespoon vegetable oil
1	tablespoon soy sauce
1	teaspoon ground ginger
1	teaspoon Dijon mustard
1	green onion, chopped
1	cooked deli-barbecued chicken, quartered
	Rice (optional)

Combine sauce ingredients in blender, mix until smooth.
Place chicken, skin side down, in shallow baking pan.
Spoon 1/2 the sauce over chicken.
Turn over and spoon on remaining sauce.
Bake uncovered in 475 degree oven 10 minutes, baste once.
Serve with cooked rice, if desired.

Serves 3

Roz Sherman

Sherried Chicken in Orange Sauce

Nothing compares to the pleasure of eating this roasted chicken, with the addition of home-style vegetables, and a sauce that's good to the very last drop.

1/2	**cup flour**
	Pepper to taste
	Paprika to taste
2	**(3 pound) chickens, cut up**
1/4	**cup margarine, melted**
2	**large onions, sliced**
1/2	**cup chopped green pepper**
1	**cup sliced mushrooms**
2	**tablespoons cornstarch**
3	**tablespoons water**
2	**cups orange juice**
1/4	**cup sherry**
3	**tablespoons brown sugar**
2	**teaspoons grated orange zest**

Combine flour, pepper and paprika in a paper bag.
Add chicken, 1 or 2 pieces at a time, shake to coat, shaking off excess.
Arrange chicken in a 13 x 9-inch baking dish.

Melt margarine, sauté onions, peppers and mushrooms.
Spread over chicken.
In sauce pan, stir cornstarch into water, blending until smooth.
Combine with remaining ingredients, blend again.
Simmer over low heat until thickened, pour over chicken.
Bake uncovered in 375 degree oven 1 hour.

Serves 8

Harriet Kruman

Skillet Roasted Lemon Chicken with Potatoes

Highly seasoned with olives and herbs makes this dish rich and flavorful. Use Mediterranean or Kalamata olives for best taste.

3	teaspoons extra virgin olive oil, divided
1	large lemon, sliced
1/2	teaspoon grated lemon zest
1	tablespoon fresh lemon juice
1/2	teaspoon salt, divided
1/4	teaspoon pepper, divided
6	garlic cloves, minced, divided
8	(3 ounce) chicken breasts, skinless, boneless
1	teaspoon fresh chopped rosemary (or 1/4 teaspoon dried)
10	cherry tomatoes
10	Kalamata olives
1	pound (8) small red potatoes, quartered
1	zucchini, sliced
1	small onion, chopped

Coat a 10-inch cast iron skillet with 1 teaspoon oil.
Arrange lemon slices in a single layer on bottom of skillet.
Combine 1 teaspoon oil, lemon zest, lemon juice, 1/4 teaspoon salt, 1/8 teaspoon pepper and 4 garlic cloves in large bowl.
Add chicken and toss to coat.
Place chicken in single layer on top of lemon slices.

Combine 1 teaspoon oil with remaining ingredients, toss to coat, arrange over chicken.
Bake in 450 degree oven 1 hour or until chicken is cooked.

Serves 4

Florie Krell

Spice-Rubbed Sticky Chicken

You'll love this combination of spices. A quick and easy way to add high flavor. The fabulous smell of this chicken cooking will bring all the neighborhood children to you back door for dinner!

Dry Herb Rub:

2	teaspoons salt
1	teaspoon paprika
3/4	teaspoon cayenne pepper
1/2	teaspoon onion powder
1/2	teaspoon thyme
1/2	teaspoon white pepper
1/4	teaspoon garlic powder
1/4	teaspoon black pepper
1	(3 pound) chicken
1	onion, chopped

Preheat oven to 250 degrees.
Mix dry herbs together. Rub inside and outside of chicken.
Refrigerate overnight.
Fill cavity of chicken with chopped onion.
Roast covered, 3 1/2 hours or until done, basting chicken with juices.

Serves 4

Nancy Neudorf

Hint:
Herb bread: add chopped herbs to biscuit or bread dough.

Thai Chicken

Authentically seasoned and colorful-perfect party fare. Fresh lemon grass can be found in one of the Asian groceries.

1	stalk lemon grass, sliced and macerated
2	small garlic cloves, chopped
3	tablespoons chopped parsley
1	tablespoon ground coriander
2	teaspoons sugar
1	teaspoon chili oil
1 1/2	pounds chicken breasts, boneless, cut in thin strips
2	tablespoons peanut oil
1	teaspoon sesame oil
1	carrot, julienned
1/2-1	medium onion, chopped coarsely
1	cup lettuce, coarsely chopped
	Rice

(Prepare all ingredients before beginning to cook.)
Combine first 6 ingredients and mash with a mortar and pestle.
Stir-fry chicken in peanut oil and sesame oil. Remove when cooked.

Stir-fry carrots, then onions, then lettuce. (Add more oil if necessary.)
Add chicken and mashed spices.
Stir-fry together 2 to 3 minutes (do not over cook).
Serve immediately over rice.

Serves 4

Ruth Fauman-Fichman

Ground Turkey and Black Bean Chili

A hearty meal that tastes just as good the second day - if there is any left.

1	tablespoon olive oil
2	cups chopped red peppers
1	cup chopped onion
1/2	cup chopped carrot
2	cloves garlic, minced
4	teaspoons chili powder
2	teaspoons ground cumin
1	pound ground turkey
2	(16 ounce) cans black beans, drained and rinsed
3	cups chicken broth
1	(6 ounce) can tomato paste

Sauté peppers, onion, carrot and garlic in oil, 10 minutes.
Add chili powder and cumin, mix well.
Add ground turkey, sauté until brown.
Add beans, chicken broth and tomato paste.
Simmer 1 hour, stirring occasionally.

Serves 4

Marianne Silberman

Hint:

Beans: when cooking dried beans, add salt after cooking. If added at the start, it will slow the cooking process.

Turkey with Wild Rice, Almonds and Mushrooms

A delicious way to serve leftover turkey. Don't wait until Thanksgiving to try this recipe.

1/2	cup chopped onion
1/2	cup chopped celery
1/4	cup margarine
1/4	cup flour
1	chicken bouillon cube
1	cup hot water
1	(8 ounce) can mushrooms, drained (reserve liquid)
1 1/2	cups nondairy creamer (or less)
3	cups cubed cooked turkey or chicken
1	cup wild or white rice
1	tablespoon pimento (optional)
1	tablespoon parsley flakes
	Salt and pepper to taste
1/2	cup slivered almonds (garnish)

In large saucepan sauté onion and celery in margarine until tender.
Blend in flour. Dissolve bouillon cube in boiling water.
Add bouillon, mushroom liquid and nondairy substitute to flour mixture.
Stir until blended and thickened (about 1 minute).

Add remaining ingredients (except almonds). Mix well, pour into 2 quart casserole.
Bake covered, in 350 degree oven, 45 minutes.
Sprinkle almonds on top, bake 15 minutes more.

Serves 4 to 6

Beverly Robins

Upside-Down Roasted Turkey
with Honey-Wine Marinade

A superb sauce or basting liquid for an unforgettable turkey. A rich gravy is made directly in the pan combining the marinade and the turkey essence that forms while the bird is roasting.

Marinade:

1	cup soy sauce
1	cup sherry
1	bay leaf
1	cup white wine
2	cloves garlic, chopped
3/4	cup honey
1/2	tablespoon poultry seasoning
1	onion, coarsely chopped
1/2	tablespoon dried rosemary, chopped

Turkey (any size):

2	tablespoons olive oil
2	tablespoons peanut oil

Combine marinade ingredients, boil 5 minutes. Cool completely.
In a large plastic bag, pour marinade over turkey and refrigerate 24 hours.
Two hours before roasting bring turkey to room temperature.
Stuff turkey with your favorite stuffing.

Pour reserved marinade in bottom of roasting pan.
Place turkey on a rack and rub with peanut and olive oils.
Roast in a 325 degree oven, breast side down, uncovered, 1 1/2 hours.
Turn over, tent with foil, roast 15 minutes per pound, baste often.

Yields (depends on turkey size)

Dee Selekman

MEATS
MEATS
MEATS

MEATS

Chili con Carne

Looking for the perfect Super Bowl Sunday supper...here it is! This can be doubled or tripled, made in advance and heated quickly.

2	tablespoons oil
1	medium onion, minced
2	celery ribs, minced
1/3	green pepper, minced
1	pound ground beef
1	(4 ounce) can mushrooms (optional)
1	(8 ounce) can tomato sauce
1	(10 1/2 ounce) can tomato soup, undiluted
3/4	cup water
1/2	teaspoon chili powder
1/2	teaspoon salt
1/2	teaspoon pepper
1/2	teaspoon garlic powder
1	(14 ounce) can kidney beans, drained

Sauté in oil, onion, celery and pepper.
Remove with slotted spoon and set aside.
Brown the beef, drain, add remaining ingredients except kidney beans.
Simmer about 2 hours, add kidney beans and heat.
Serve hot over rice or macaroni.

Serves 3 to 4

Rhoda Judd

Hint:

Meatballs: shape meatballs and hamburgers very gently, do not compact. This will keep ground meat mixture light and moist.

Grilled London Broil with Balsamic Glaze

Preparing this meal is easy and leaves plenty of time for clean-up before dinner.
A black tie dinner entrée you can enjoy in blue jeans.

1	(3 pound) Newport Roast, butterflied (see Note)

Marinade:

1/2	cup soy sauce
2	tablespoons salad oil
1/3	cup Balsamic vinegar
1/4	cup molasses (optional)
2	tablespoons brown sugar
4	cloves garlic, minced
2	slices fresh ginger, minced
1	teaspoon rosemary
1	teaspoon dried thyme
1	teaspoon fresh pepper
1/2	teaspoon salt
1	tablespoon onion flakes
2	tablespoons chopped fresh parsley

Whisk together marinade ingredients.
Poke holes in meat and score both sides crisscross 1/8-inch deep.
Combine meat and marinade in an extra large zip top plastic bag.
Refrigerate overnight turning 2 or 3 times.

Grill meat until medium rare, about 7 minutes each side.
Let meat rest 5 minutes, slice very thin.

Note: A Newport Roast is also known as a 'Spenser Roast' cut from the chuck
shoulder.
Beef may be cut into 1 1/2-inch cubes for kabobs.

Serves 6 to 8

Sheila Glasser

Picadillo

Picadillo (pronounced 'pick-a-de-yo') is a Cuban ground beef dish eaten over rice. It can be used as a filling for enchiladas, tacos, tostados and the like.

1	**tablespoon olive oil**
3	**cloves garlic, minced**
1/2	**cup finely chopped onion**
1/2	**green bell pepper, finely chopped**
1	**pound ground beef**
1/4	**cup pimento-stuffed green olives, finely chopped**
1/4	**cup white raisins**
2	**tablespoons drained capers**
1/2	**cup dry white wine**
1/2	**cup tomato sauce**
	Salt and pepper to taste
1	**teaspoon cumin powder**

Heat oil in a large frying pan over medium-high heat.
Add garlic, onion and green pepper, cook until soft but not brown, about 3 minutes.

Add ground beef, cook about 2 minutes until no longer pink.
Stir in olives, raisins and capers, cook for 2 minutes.
Stir in wine and tomato sauce, reduce heat.

Simmer 10 minutes, until beef is cooked and most of the liquid has evaporated. (The Picadillo should be moist but not soupy.)
Correct seasoning, adding salt, pepper and cumin to taste.

Serves 4

Dorita Krifcher

Roasted Beef Brisket in Barbecue Sauce

Chopped vegetables, herb and spices add to the flavor of this tender dish. More than barbecued meat, this is an elegant dinner.

3	pounds beef brisket or French roast
1 1/2	cups water
1/2	cup chopped onions
2	tablespoons minced garlic
1	cup ketchup
3	tablespoons vinegar
2	tablespoons fresh lemon juice
2	tablespoons brown sugar
1 1/2	tablespoons sweet and tangy steak sauce
2	teaspoons cornstarch
1 1/2	teaspoons paprika
1	teaspoon chili powder
1	teaspoon red pepper flakes
1/4	teaspoon liquid smoke (optional)

Place meat in large roaster with 1/2 cup of water. Reserve 1 cup.
Cover and bake in a 325 degree oven 1 1/2 hours.

Sauté onions and garlic, add next 9 ingredients plus remaining water.
Simmer 10 minutes, then add liquid smoke. Set aside. (May double sauce.)

Remove meat from oven, drain off fat, pour sauce over meat.
Bake 1 1/2 hours longer or until tender. Slice meat on the diagonal.

Serves 8

Jessy Stein

Shredded Beef on a Bun with Spicy Barbecue Sauce

These wondrously succulent barbecued sandwiches are something out of the ordinary and a guaranteed crowd pleaser.

1	**(6 pound) boneless chuck roast, cut into 6 pieces**
3-4	**celery ribs, chopped**
3-4	**green onions, chopped**
1	**green pepper, chopped**
1	**(28 ounce) bottle ketchup**
3	**tablespoons prepared barbecue sauce**
1 1/2	**cups water**
3	**tablespoons vinegar**
1	**teaspoon Tabasco sauce**
2	**tablespoons chili powder**
2	**tablespoons salt**
1	**teaspoon pepper**
	Sandwich buns

Combine all ingredients and pour over roast.
Bring to boil on top of stove.
Cover, bake in a 300 degree oven 6 hours.
When cool, shred meat, serve on buns.

Note: I use only Open Pit Barbecue Sauce for this recipe.

Makes 40 sandwiches

Gail Heiss

Hints:

Roasts: Always have your meat at room temperature before cooking, or your timing may be off. This is particularly important for roasts to be cooked rare to pink.

Union Grill "Home-Cooked" Meatloaf

If you've never served meatloaf at a party try this one. It will wow your guests. This is a favorite at our restaurant, and brings back memories of Mom, home and great food.

2	eggs, lightly beaten
1	large onion, minced
2	teaspoons seasoning salt
1	tablespoon garlic powder
2	teaspoons onion powder
1 1/2	teaspoons black pepper
1	tablespoon Worcestershire sauce
1/3	cup ketchup
1	tablespoon Dijon mustard
2	pounds ground chuck
2	cups fresh bread crumbs

Preheat oven 350 degrees.

Mix all ingredients together except ground chuck and bread crumbs. Mix well.

Add beef and mix, almost kneading (should look real moist).

Add 1 1/2 cups bread crumbs and stir. (Add remainder of bread crumbs if too moist.)

Place into 9 x 5-inch loaf pan. Bake about 1 hour, until brown and firm.

Serves 6

Compliments of Chef Victor Tome
Union Grill Restaurant

Hint:

Fresh herbs: for fresh herbs, use ⅓ the amount of dried. Dried herbs are more concentrated.

Mushroom Crusted Lamb with Leek Puree

The different types of mushrooms make this an enticing blend of tastes and textures. It's a recipe with a lot of steps, but the delicious result is worth the extra effort.

Leek Puree:

2	leeks, chopped (tough green tops trimmed)
	Water to cover
	Salt and pepper to taste
1	teaspoon margarine
2	cloves minced garlic
2	cups assorted fresh wild mushrooms (enoki, morel, shiitake, etc.)
1	teaspoon crushed rosemary
1	teaspoon olive oil
2	ounces dried mushrooms (trumpet, wood ear, porcini, etc.)
2	boneless (4 to 6 ribs) racks of lamb
1/2	cup flour
1	egg, beaten
1	teaspoon extra virgin olive oil

Preheat oven to 500 degrees.
Combine all leek puree ingredients in saucepan, boil 5 to 7 minutes, until soft. Set aside, keep warm.
Sauté garlic, fresh mushrooms and rosemary in oil, set aside, keep warm.

Coarsely grind dry mushrooms in blender.
Dip lamb into flour then egg, coat with mushroom mixture.
Sear lamb in oil over high heat, remove.
Bake on rack 4 minutes for rare, 6 minutes medium rare.
Cut into 1-inch slices.

To serve, spread leek puree in center of dish, top with lamb slices.
Spoon sautéed fresh mushrooms alongside.

Serves 4

Compliments of Brad Samuels
Washington, DC

New Zealand Rack of Lamb

This cut of meat needs nothing more than the traditional coating of parsley, thyme and basil, salt and pepper. The raspberry-lime sauce adds the final perfect touch.

1	(10 ounce) package frozen raspberries, thawed
2	teaspoons fresh lime juice
1/4	cup sugar
2	(8 to 10 ounce) rack baby lamb, French cut
1	teaspoon minced fresh parsley
1	teaspoon minced fresh thyme
1	teaspoon minced fresh basil
	Salt and fresh ground pepper to taste
1	lime, cut in half into a crown (garnish)

In blender or food processor puree raspberries.
Strain out seeds, stir in lime juice. Add sugar to taste.

Preheat oven to 425 degrees.
Combine parsley, thyme and basil, rub 1/2 of mixture into lamb.
Season with salt and pepper. Place lamb on rack, roast 30 minutes.

Remove, sprinkle remainder of herbs and small amount of sauce on both sides of meat.
Return to oven, finish cooking, about 15 minutes more for rare.
Place sauce on plates, top with lamb, garnish with lime.

Serves 2

Compliments of LeMont Restaurant

Moré Veal Daniela

Sun-dried tomatoes, pignoli nuts and hearts of palm create colorful, elegant veal medallions. This is one of our favorites.

12	small pieces veal (or chicken), pounded thin, dusted with flour
4	tablespoons olive oil
2	tablespoons sun-dried tomatoes
2	tablespoons pignoli nuts
2	tablespoons sliced mushrooms (cooked)
4	tablespoons white wine
4	tablespoons margarine, cut up
4	pieces hearts of palm, sliced
	Parsley (garnish)

In large skillet, heat olive oil, sauté all veal about 5 minutes, until cooked. Drain excess oil and return pan to stove.

Add all ingredients and heat to boiling point. (If too thick, add some water.) Garnish with chopped parsley and serve.

Serves 2

Compliments of Chef Louie Moré
Moré Restaurant

Mushroom Stuffed Breast of Veal with Vegetable Pan Gravy

A skillful combination of complementing flavors. A classic, especially for holidays and a delicious change of pace.

2	tablespoons oil
3	large onions, sliced (3 cups)
8	ounces fresh mushrooms, cut up
4	celery ribs, chopped
2 1/2	cups matzo meal
5	cups water, divided
	Salt and pepper to taste
2	eggs plus 1 egg white, slightly beaten
1	breast of veal (with pocket)
4	cloves of garlic, chopped
1	tablespoon oil
1	teaspoon salt
1/2	teaspoon paprika
2	tomatoes, chopped
3	green peppers, chopped

Sauté in oil, 2 cups onions, mushrooms and 1 cup celery.
Combine matzo meal with 2 cups water, salt, pepper and eggs, mix well.
Add sautéed vegetables to matzo meal, fill veal pocket and secure both ends.

Rub veal with garlic, oil, salt, paprika.
Place remaining onions, celery, tomatoes and green peppers in large roaster.
Add 3 cups of water.
Place veal on top of vegetables, cover tightly with aluminum foil.
Roast in a 450 degree oven 10 minutes.
Lower heat to 350 degrees, roast 2 3/4 hours longer.
Uncover, baste and let brown for 10 more minutes.
Let roast stand 20 minutes before serving.

Serves 6 to 8

Libby Stern

Veal and Tomato Stew with Mushrooms

Slowly simmered veal, tomatoes, and chopped vegetables, along with herbs and spices, becomes succulent perfection.

1 1/2	**pounds veal, cubed**
1	**tablespoon oil**
1	**onion, chopped**
1	**clove garlic, minced**
1	**tablespoon flour**
2	**cups chicken broth**
1	**cup canned tomatoes**
1	**tablespoon lemon juice**
1/4	**teaspoon oregano**
1/4	**teaspoon salt**
1/4	**teaspoon pepper**
1/2	**pound fresh mushrooms, sliced**

Brown veal in oil, add onion and garlic, sauté 5 minutes, set aside.
Combine remaining ingredients (except mushrooms) in saucepan, bring to boil.
Pour over veal, cover, simmer 1 hour.
Add mushrooms and cook for 30 minutes longer.

Serves 6

Marianne Silberman

Hint:

Tomatoes: keep tomatoes in storage with stems pointed downward and they will retain their freshness longer.

Veal Meatloaf with Red Bell Pepper and Spinach

What could make a meatloaf a cut above the rest? Combine veal, fresh baby spinach, onions and Dijon mustard. The flavors of the roasted red peppers are intensified by fresh basil, thyme and garlic.

2	tablespoons olive oil
1/2	(6 ounce) package fresh baby spinach
2	cups chopped onions
2	tablespoons minced garlic
2	cups fresh bread crumbs (made from French bread)
2	large eggs
1/2	cup fresh basil, chopped
6	tablespoons ketchup
2	tablespoons fresh thyme, chopped
1	tablespoon Dijon mustard
1	tablespoon prepared steak sauce
1 1/2	teaspoons salt
1/2	teaspoon ground black pepper
1	large red bell pepper, roasted, peeled, sliced into 1/2-inch strips
2	pounds ground veal

Add 1 tablespoon oil to skillet over medium high heat.
Add spinach, toss until just wilted. Set aside.
Add remaining oil to skillet, sauté onions and garlic 5 minutes.
In a large bowl, combine remaining ingredients (except peppers and veal).
Add onions, mix in veal.

Place 1/2 of veal mixture in 9 x 5-inch metal loaf pan.
Using back of spoon, make a 1-inch wide, 1/2-inch deep canal lengthwise down middle of loaf.
Lay 1/2 of red pepper strips in canal, then spinach and remaining peppers.
Fill pan with remaining veal mixture, press firmly.
Bake in a 350 degree oven 50 minutes and brown on top.
Cool 15 minutes. Serve in slices.

Serves 6 to 8

Sheila Glasser

PASTA, POTATOES AND RICE

Pasta, Potatoes and Rice

Chilled Pasta with Peanut Sauce and Snow Peas

A tasty noodle dish that has become popular in upscale restaurants. Luckily, it's easy to make at home.

1	pound thin spaghetti, broken, cooked and drained
2	teaspoons sesame oil
2	tablespoons peanut butter
2	tablespoons white vinegar (or rice vinegar)
2	teaspoons soy sauce
	Hot chili sauce to taste
2	tablespoons sherry
1/2	teaspoon sugar
3/4	cup carrots, julienned
3/4	cup snow peas, julienned
1/4	cup unsalted peanuts, chopped

Toss spaghetti with sesame oil, set aside.
In a mixing bowl, combine peanut butter, vinegar, soy sauce, chili sauce, sherry and sugar.
Stir together until smooth.

Blanch carrots and snow peas in boiling water.
Drain, refresh under running water.
Add vegetables and peanuts to the pasta.
Pour peanut sauce on top, toss and refrigerate.

Serves 4

Compliments of Bob Schnarrenberger
Paper Moon Chef Services

Farfalle Pasta with Pignoli Nuts and Sun-Dried Tomatoes

Just a short while ago, it seemed that no one outside of Italy had heard of sun-dried tomatoes. Now they are everywhere! Sun-dried tomatoes have a strong piquant flavor and are often salty- use them sparingly.

1/3	cup olive oil
2	cloves garlic, minced
3-4	small zucchini, julienned
1/2	cup sun-dried tomatoes, rinsed, dried, chopped
1/2	cup fresh basil, chopped
	Salt and fresh ground pepper to taste
1	pound bow tie pasta (Farfalle)
1/4	cup reserved pasta cooking water
3/4	cup pine nuts (Pignoli), lightly toasted
1/2	cup freshly grated Parmesan cheese

In large skillet, heat olive oil over medium heat, sauté garlic 30 seconds.
Add zucchini and tomatoes, sauté 3 to 5 minutes.
Stir in basil, salt and pepper.

Cook pasta 10 minutes, drain, reserve 1/4 cup cooking water.
Place pasta in large bowl. Add vegetables, pine nuts, cheese and water.
Toss well, serve immediately.
Pass additional grated Parmesan cheese if desired.

Serves 4, or 8 to 10 as a first course

Roz Sherman

Noodles Meprazrelian D'Malatesta

Errico Malatesta was a nice man with baggy pants and a beard. An enlightened anarchist of the previous century. Hang loose, you must concentrate on the folklore. But , it works - time tested.

1-2	**pounds wide egg noodles**
1-2	**pounds ground beef (or veal)**
	Garlic powder to taste
	Fresh mushrooms
	Sweet red wine to taste
	Canola or olive oil
1	**large red pimento, diced**
	Ketchup to taste

Cook up a generous pot of lokshn (noodles).
Drain and keep the lokshn warm—and don't let them stick to one another.
Broil (less fat) or fry (more fat) a pound or two of chopped beef or veal.
Sprinkle liberally with garlic powder before cooking.

Take a microwave safe tepple (pot).
Into it crumble mushrooms, add some kiddish wine.
Add canola or olive oil, and a big diced pimento. Cook the contents of tepple 3 minutes in microwave.
Mix with meat and some ketchup to taste.
Bed down a long corning ware pan with the lokshn.
Put meat mixture atop it.

Cover and bake in oven at 350 degrees for 1 1/2 hours.
You could jog or take a bath while waiting, but use seykl (sense).
It takes siychl not just mazel (luck) to get married, too.

Serves more or less depending on appetite

Rabbi Gershon Freidlin

Pasta with Spinach and Pine Nuts

If you're bored with ordinary spaghetti, this full-flavored spinach, robust garlic and crunchy pine nuts provide a satisfying alternative.

1/2	cup pine nuts
1/4	cup olive oil
2	large garlic cloves, minced
1/4	teaspoon red pepper flakes
1	pound spinach or escarole, chopped
1	pound spaghetti, cooked al dente
2	tablespoons butter
1/4	cup Parmesan cheese
	Salt and pepper to taste

Sauté pine nuts until golden, set aside.
In olive oil, sauté garlic and red pepper flakes 1 minute.
Add spinach, toss over high heat until wilted. Stir in butter.

Place hot, drained pasta in bowl.
Add spinach mixture, cheese and pine nuts, toss well.
Season with salt and pepper. Serve immediately.

Serves 4 to 6

Marlene Gelman

Hint:

Pasta: pasta is best when cooked just before serving. The alternative is to cook ahead of time and reheat with a simple sauce in a skillet.

Rolled Lasagna with Spinach and Mushrooms

This is a very rich pasta dish that needs only a light salad and a good Italian bread to complete the meal. It can be prepared with any fresh or store-bought sauce.

3	tablespoons butter
3	tablespoons flour
1	cup half-and-half
	Nutmeg, salt and pepper to taste

1/2	cup chopped shallots
1	clove garlic, crushed
5	tablespoons margarine or butter, divided
2	(10 ounce) packages frozen spinach, thawed, drained
1/2	pound mushrooms, chopped
2	eggs
1/4	cup grated Parmesan cheese
1/4	pound grated mozzarella cheese
1	(16 ounce) package lasagna noodles, cooked and drained
2	cups any prepared marinara sauce

Melt butter in small saucepan, add flour and stir constantly for 1 minute.
Add half-and-half, stir constantly until thick and smooth.
Add salt, pepper and nutmeg to taste. Set aside.

Sauté shallots and garlic in 3 tablespoons margarine or butter.
Add spinach, cook until dry, remove to bowl.

Sauté mushrooms in 2 tablespoons margarine or butter. Add to spinach.
Add eggs, both cheeses, mix well.
Spread a spoonful of filling on each lasagne noodle, roll up.

Cover bottom of lasagne pan with white sauce.
Place rolls in pan, cover with marinara sauce.
Bake in a 350 degree oven for 30 minutes.

Serves 8

Barbara Oleinick

Triple Cheese Penne Pasta with Shiitake Mushrooms

This simply spectacular ultra-cheesy pasta entrée is just as perfect for weekday suppers as an elegant dinner. A terrific make-ahead dish that will please everyone.

2	cups minced onion
2	large cloves garlic, minced
1	teaspoon red pepper flakes (or to taste)
1	teaspoon dried basil, crumbled
1	teaspoon dried oregano, crumbled
1	pound Shiitake mushrooms, stems discarded, caps sliced
2	tablespoons olive oil
4	tablespoons unsalted butter (reserve 1 tablespoon)
3	tablespoons flour
2	cups milk
2	(28 ounce) cans plum tomatoes, drained, chopped
1	cup (1/4 pound) Fontina cheese, grated
1	cup (1/4 pound) Gorgonzola cheese, crumbled
1 1/2	cups fresh grated Parmesan cheese (reserve 1/4 cup)
2/3	cup minced fresh parsley
1	pound Penne or Farfalle pasta
	Salt and pepper to taste

In large skillet, cook first 6 ingredients in oil over low heat until soft.
Add mushrooms, cook 10 to 15 minutes until tender.
Transfer mixture to large bowl.

In same skillet, melt 3 tablespoons butter over low heat.
Whisk in flour to make roux, stirring constantly for 3 minutes.
Add milk in a thin stream, whisk together to mix well.
Simmer, whisking 2 minutes or until thickened.
Pour sauce over mushroom mixture. Add tomatoes, cheeses and parsley.

Cook pasta in boiling water 5 minutes (will not be tender), drain thoroughly.
Add pasta, salt and pepper to mushroom mixture, combine well.
Transfer mixture to a buttered 11 x 14-inch baking dish.

(May be prepared up to this point, covered, and chilled overnight. Bring to room temperature before continuing with recipe.)
Sprinkle with remaining Parmesan cheese and butter.
Bake on middle rack at 450 degrees for 25 to 30 minutes until top is golden and pasta is soft.

Serves 4

Sema Fineberg

Cherry Noodle Kugel with Nuts and Coconut

Just when you think you've heard of every conceivable way to prepare kugels, yet another unusual and delicious recipe surfaces!

1/2	pound medium egg noodles, cooked al dente
4	eggs
1/3	cup sugar
1	teaspoon vanilla
1	(14 ounce) can sour pitted cherries, drained
4	tablespoons butter or margarine, melted
1/4	cup chopped nuts (optional)
1/4	cup shredded coconut (optional)
	Sugar and cinnamon
1	tablespoon margarine

Beat eggs, sugar and vanilla, add cherries.
Combine noodles, egg mixture, shortening and nuts, mix well.

Pour into well greased 9 x 11-inch baking dish.
Sprinkle with sugar, cinnamon and coconut.
Dot with margarine, bake at 350 degrees 40 minutes until brown.

Serves 6

Gertrude Mallinger

Hint:

Prevent boil overs: add a lump of butter or 2 teaspoons vegetable oil to water, rice, noodles or spaghetti will not boil over or stick together.

Creamy Noodle Kugel with Sliced Peaches

The traditional combination of flavors make this a very popular dish. It's particularly nice for a holiday buffet.

1	pint sour cream
1	pound creamed cottage cheese
6	eggs, beaten
1	cup margarine, melted
3/4	cup sugar
1/2	teaspoon salt
1	(16 ounce) can sliced peaches (reserve 1/4 cup juice)
1	pound wide egg noodles, cooked, drained

Topping:

1/2	cup cornflake crumbs
1/4	cup brown sugar
4	tablespoons margarine, melted

Combine all ingredients except peaches and noodles, blend well.
Add noodles, peaches and juice. (May substitute crushed pineapple.)
Pour into a greased 9 x 13-inch pan.

Combine topping ingredients, sprinkle evenly on top.
Bake uncovered in a 350 degree oven for 1 hour.

Serves 6 to 8

Submitted by Sally Samuels in memory of Shirley Bernhardt

Double Cheese and Mixed Vegetable Noodle Kugel

A very savory dish made of eggs, cheese and a variety of vegetables.

1	pound spinach noodles, cooked al dente
1	pound cottage cheese
1	cup grated Cheddar cheese
2	eggs, lightly beaten
4	tablespoons butter or oil
1/2	teaspoon garlic salt
1	teaspoon tarragon
1/2	teaspoon dry mustard
	Pepper to taste
1	bunch broccoli, steamed, diced
1/2	head cauliflower, steamed, diced
1	onion, sliced, sautéed
1/2	red pepper, diced, sautéed

Topping:

6-8	mushrooms, sliced, sautéed
1/2	cup grated Cheddar cheese

Mix all ingredients together except topping. Pour into a greased 9 x 13-inch pan.
Top with mushrooms and Cheddar cheese.
Bake in a 350 degree oven 30 minutes or until cheese bubbles and browns.

Serves 8

Marlene Gelman

Sweet and Silky Noodle Soufflé

This noodle soufflé is one of the most scrumptious ever. The combination of the smooth rich flavors of half-and-half and evaporated milk are the secret to this dish. The addition of peaches and raisins make this an elegant presentation.

1	**(12 ounce) package wide egg noodles, cooked and drained**
11	**ounces cream cheese**
1	**(14 ounce) can sliced peaches, drained**
1/2	**cup raisins**
8	**eggs**
3/4	**cup sugar**
1	**teaspoon vanilla**
2	**(12 ounce) cans evaporated milk**
2	**cups half-and-half**
1	**teaspoon cinnamon**

Preheat oven to 375 degrees.
Spoon noodles into a well buttered 11 x 13-inch baking dish.
Cut cream cheese into small squares, scatter on top of noodles.
Spread peaches and raisins on top of noodles.

Beat eggs with sugar, vanilla, evaporated milk and half-and-half.
Pour custard mixture on top, sprinkle with cinnamon.
Bake for 40 minutes or until toothpick placed in center comes out clean.

Note: May be prepared 1 or 2 days in advance, refrigerate (do not freeze). Bring to room temperature, then bake.

Serves 12

Compliments of Lila Grushka Catering
Tucson, Arizona

Cheddar Baked Potatoes
with Parmesan Cheese and Herbs

Imagine gooey cheeses melting into a just-baked potato, sprinkled with butter and herbs make this a satisfying accompaniment.

4	medium potatoes
3	tablespoons fresh herbs (your choice) or 3 teaspoons dried
1	teaspoon salt
3	tablespoons melted butter
4-6	tablespoons grated Cheddar cheese
1 1/2	tablespoons Parmesan cheese

Cut potatoes across into thin slices (not all the way through).
Place potatoes in baking dish and fan slightly to separate.
Combine all herbs together.
Season potato with salt, drizzle butter, top with herbs.

Bake potatoes in a 425 degree oven 40 minutes.
Remove from oven, sprinkle with cheeses.
Return to oven, bake 10 to 15 minutes longer until browned and cheese melted.
May prepare ahead and bake before serving.

Serves 4

Sheila Glasser

Hints:
Potatoes: a few drops of lemon juice or vinegar in the water will whiten potatoes.

Chunky Mashed Potatoes and Parsnips

This mixture of parsnips and potato is delicious and sweet. It compliments everything from fish to beef.

1 1/2	pounds russet potatoes
1	pound parsnips
3/4	cup chicken broth
1/2	teaspoon salt
1/8	teaspoon pepper
1/4	cup half-and-half or nondairy creamer
3	tablespoons margarine

Cut potatoes and parsnips into 2-inch cubes.
Place in ovenproof 2 quart casserole.
Add chicken broth, salt and pepper.
Bake in a 450 degree oven 45 minutes.
Remove from oven, add cream and butter.
Mash with potato masher, leaving potatoes and parsnips chunky.

Serves 6

Marianne Silberman

Oven-Browned New Potatoes with Garlic and Rosemary

The flavor of the garlic intensifies as you cook and is delicious spread on fresh buttered bread.

1 1/2	pounds small red potatoes
10-12	garlic cloves, unpeeled and flattened
2	tablespoons olive oil
1/2	tablespoon crumbled dried rosemary (heaping)
	Salt and fresh ground pepper to taste

Preheat over to 450 degrees.
Cut potatoes into 1 1/4-inch wedges.
Combine all ingredients in a 9 x 13-inch baking dish in a single layer.
Roast 45 minutes, stirring every 15 minutes, until tender and browned.
Remove garlic, squeeze from skin, spread on bread.

Serves 4

Ruth Fauman-Fichman

Classic Potato Kugel

One of life's great temptations is potato kugel. This is the granddaddy of all potato dishes and is a traditional side dish to anything!

8-10	**potatoes**
1	**onion, grated**
2	**cloves of garlic, grated**
3-4	**eggs, beaten**
3/4	**cup flour**
1	**teaspoon baking powder**
	Salt and pepper to taste
8	**tablespoons melted shortening, divided (or more)**
	Paprika

Grate potatoes, squeeze out liquid. Add onion, garlic and eggs.
Blend in flour and baking powder (this keeps it from getting dark).
Add salt and pepper, and 4 tablespoons melted shortening.
(Batter should not be runny.)

Place 2 tablespoons oil in each of 2 (8 x 8-inch) baking pans.
Heat on top of stove burner until shortening bubbles.
Pour a drop of batter into pan to see if it cooks quickly.
(Kugel will stick to pan if shortening is not hot enough.)
Pour in batter, sprinkle with paprika.
Bake in a 350 degree oven 1 hour or more until brown.

Note: Use enough shortening to rise up around the batter when you pour it into the pan. This will make a wonderful crispy crust. Increase baking time for additional potatoes. Longer cooking time produces a crispier kugel.

Serves 10 to 12

Ruth Ganz Fargotstein

Creamy Mashed Potatoes In Advance

There is nothing more comforting than a large serving of hot fluffy mashed potatoes. This is a special favorite of my daughter, Staci. This recipe is easily reheatable, has marvelous soufflé texture and unbelievable taste!

5-6	medium potatoes, peeled and quartered
	Water
2	tablespoons margarine, softened
1/4	cup milk
1	(3 ounce) package cream cheese, softened
3/4	cup sour cream
1	tablespoon chopped chives
1/4	teaspoon garlic salt
1/2	teaspoon onion salt
	Fresh pepper to taste

Cook potatoes in water to cover, 15 minutes or until fork tender, drain. Mash potatoes with soft butter with electric mixer on low speed. Beat in remaining ingredients and serve.

Note: May be prepared 2 days ahead and refrigerated.
To heat, microwave at full power, covered, 8 to 10 minutes.

Serves 6

Sheila Glasser

Hint:

Potato Pancakes: when making potato pancakes, add a little sour cream to keep potatoes from discoloring.

Parmesan Potato Wedges

Very quick and easy to make, the Parmesan cheese highlights the subtle taste of the potato.

1	large baking potato, cut into quarters, lengthwise
	Vegetable spray
	Salt and pepper to taste
	Oregano to taste
1/2	cup grated Parmesan cheese

Place the potato wedges in pot of cold water, bring to a boil.
Adjust to simmer, cook until the wedges are just tender.
Carefully remove them from the water, allow to drain, dry, cool.

Spray each wedge and season to taste.
Spray again, dip each wedge into grated cheese.
(A slightly heavy coat of cheese should coat the potato.)
Place wedges on baking sheet, bake in 350 degree oven, 20 minutes or until golden.

Serves 2

Compliments of Richard Amster
Feature Food Writer, The Jewish Chronicle

Potato Basil Gratin

Sometimes the best way to describe a dish is by its smell rather than the way it tastes. This aromatic dish combines the pungent, savory scent of fresh basil with the earthy, inviting smell of roasted potatoes.

5	tablespoons extra virgin olive oil
12-15	cloves garlic, sliced thin
1	bunch of basil (the best is small-leafed)
6	medium-sized potatoes, sliced thin
	Salt and pepper to taste

Pour 2 tablespoons of olive oil into 8 x 11-inch baking dish.
Add 1/2 the garlic and basil, cover well with one layer of potatoes.
Place the remaining garlic, basil and potatoes in layers into dish.
Season each layer with salt and pepper.
Pour remaining 3 tablespoons of olive oil over the mixture.
Bake in a 425 degree oven approximately 35 minutes.

Serves 6 to 8

Myra Judd

Hint:

Dull seasoning: cooling or chilling dulls the flavor of any seasoning. For this reason, any salad, cold soup or cold vegetable needs to be liberally seasoned before serving. Remember to be generous with salt and pepper.

Mashed Sweet Potatoes with Balsamic Vinegar

Gently spiced and sweetly tart, this is mashed potatoes elegant cousin.

4-5	(4 pounds) sweet potatoes, scrubbed
2	tablespoons butter
1/8	teaspoon ground cinnamon
1/8	teaspoon freshly grated nutmeg
1	cup milk
1	teaspoon salt
	Freshly ground pepper to taste
1-2	teaspoons balsamic vinegar

Bake sweet potatoes 50 minutes or until easily pierced with a paring knife.
Allow potatoes to cool just enough to handle.
Peel and pass through a food mill or ricer, set aside.

In medium saucepan, heat butter over low heat until golden.
Stir in cinnamon and nutmeg.
Remove from heat, stir in milk, return and bring to a boil.
Add to sweet potato puree, stir with a wooden spoon to combine thoroughly.
Season with salt and pepper, stir in balsamic vinegar.

Note: Use more or less of the balsamic vinegar to vary tartness of potatoes.

Serves 4

Ilene Fingeret

Tender Roasted Sweet Potatoes and Onions

Something both colorful and different. These potatoes are so rich you'll swear they're coated in butter.

4	medium sweet potatoes, cut in 2-inch pieces
2	medium sweet onions, cut in 1-inch pieces
2	tablespoons canola or olive oil
3/4	teaspoon garlic-pepper blend
1/2	teaspoon salt

Preheat oven to 425 degrees.
Combine all ingredients in a 13 x 9-inch baking dish, toss to coat.
Bake 35 minutes or until tender, stirring occasionally.

Serves 6

Loraine Newman Mackler

Cuban Style Black Beans and Rice

The combination of beans and rice makes a complete protein. Nutritionally it is just as good as a piece of chicken. This bean dish is very moist.

1	**pound dried black beans, picked through and washed**
1	**large onion, cut in half**
4	**cloves garlic**
2	**bay leaves**
1/2	**green bell pepper**
1	**teaspoon ground cumin**
1	**teaspoon dried oregano**

Sofrito:

1	**tablespoon olive oil**
1/2	**large onion, finely chopped**
2	**cloves garlic, minced**
1/2	**green bell pepper, finely chopped**

Seasonings:

2	**tablespoons dry white wine**
	Red wine vinegar to taste
1/2	**teaspoon sugar**
	Salt and black pepper to taste

Cooked rice

Soak beans overnight in water to cover (see Note).

To beans and water, add next 6 ingredients.
Bring to a boil over high heat. Skim.
Reduce heat, cover, simmer, stirring occasionally, for 1 hour, until soft.
Add water as necessary to keep beans submerged.
Remove onion, garlic, bay leaves and green pepper, discard.

Sauté Sofrito ingredients until cooked, stir into beans.
Cover, simmer beans until very soft, about 30 minutes.
Add seasonings to taste. Spoon beans over rice.

Note: Add about 1 hour to the cooking time if not soaking overnight. For thicker consistency, puree 1 cup of cooked beans and return to pot.

Serves 8 to 10

Dorita Krifcher

Curried Rice and Noodles

From the first forkful to the last bite, this combination of high-powered curry, rice, noodles and toasted pignoli nuts will add flair to any menu.

3	tablespoons margarine
1	small onion, finely chopped
1	large rib celery, thinly sliced
1/2	cup thin noodles, broken up
2	teaspoons curry powder
1	cup rice, uncooked
2	heaping teaspoons instant chicken broth
2	cups hot water
1/2	cup currants or golden raisins (optional)
1/4	cup pignoli nuts, toasted (optional)
	Parsley (garnish)

Melt margarine, sauté onion, celery and noodles until tender and light brown. Stir in curry powder and rice, stir for 5 minutes.

Dissolve instant soup in hot water. Add raisins, combine with rice.

Cook covered 20 minutes. Garnish with nuts and parsley.

Serves 4 to 6

Marlene Gelman

Hint:

Fluffy rice: rice will be fluffier and whiter if you add 1 teaspoon of lemon juice to each quart of water.

Egyptian Rice and Lentils

This can be main dish (especially for vegetarians or people who are trying to reduce their meat consumption) or a great side. Serve it in a shallow bowl or platter surrounded by fresh tomato wedges. I strongly recommend low-fat yogurt as an accompaniment. It keeps well and can be made ahead.

1	**cup (6 ounces) brown lentils, washed and picked over**
3/4	**teaspoon salt, divided**
1	**tablespoon plus 1 1/2 teaspoons olive oil**
1	**large onion, 1/2 chopped and 1/2 thinly sliced**
1	**tablespoon cumin seed, crushed**
1/2	**teaspoon ground cinnamon**
1/2	**cup long grain rice**
2	**cups water**
	Freshly ground pepper to taste
1	**cup plain low fat yogurt (topping)**

Cover lentils with 2-inches of water, bring to a boil.
Add 1/2 teaspoon salt, reduce heat, simmer 30 minutes, until just tender.

In another casserole, sauté chopped onion in 1 tablespoon of the olive oil until golden.
Add cumin and cinnamon, stir, add rice, stir to coat.
Add water, lentils with liquid, 1/4 teaspoon salt and pepper to taste.
Stir together, bring to a boil, reduce heat, cover.
Cook 20 to 25 minutes or until liquid is absorbed.

Brown sliced onion in remaining 1 1/2 teaspoons of olive oil.
(To really get them caramelized, use butter and a low heat.)
When the rice and lentils are cooked, transfer to a platter.
Scatter onions over top. Serve hot or cold.

Serves 4 to 6

Marla Papernick

Fried Brown Rice and Vegetables

Preparations for this colorful dish are easy and can be done a day ahead. The last-minute stir-frying takes only minutes.

1	cup brown rice, uncooked
3	tablespoons oil, divided
1	cup thinly sliced carrots
3	green sliced onions
1	clove garlic, crushed
1	large green pepper, cut in thin strips
1	cup thinly sliced zucchini
1	cup thinly sliced mushrooms
1/2	cup slivered almonds
1-6	tablespoons soy sauce

Cook rice according to package directions, omitting salt, chill.
Heat 1 tablespoon oil over high heat, add carrots, stir-fry 1 minute.
Add onions, garlic and peppers, stir-fry 1 minute (add more oil as needed.)
Add zucchini, mushrooms and almonds, stir-fry 2 minutes longer.
Add rice and stir in soy sauce to taste.

Serves 4

Terri Cohen

Orange Wild Rice with Pecans and Raisins

Exotic. An excellent cold luncheon dish.

1	cup wild rice
4	cups water
1	cup pecan halves
1	cup yellow raisins
4	green onions, sliced
2	tablespoons chopped mint
1/4	cup olive oil
1/3	cup orange juice

Cook rice in water uncovered for 30 to 40 minutes until soft, drain.
Add remaining ingredients and stir. Serve at room temperature.

Serves 4 to 6

Barbara Oleinick

My Mother's Lemon Rice

My mother has made this dish for years and everyone asks for the recipe.
Although mine never tastes quite like hers, this is how she claims it is made.

1/2	cup butter
1	clove garlic, crushed
2	cups converted rice
2 1/4	cups water and vegetable broth (50 percent of each)
2	tablespoons lemon juice
1	tablespoon grated lemon zest
1	tablespoon chopped parsley

Early in the day, place butter in saucepan with crushed garlic, set aside.
(The flavor of the garlic will permeate the butter, no need to mix.)

Remove garlic, combine rice, water, broth and butter.
Simmer until all liquid is absorbed, 20 minutes.
Remove from heat.
Stir in lemon juice, lemon zest and parsley. Serve immediately.

Serves 6

Marla Papernick

Rice with Mushrooms and Pistachios

Not only does this sophisticated recipe have an awesome mushroom and
pistachio seasoning, it's easy to cook.

1	tablespoon margarine
1/2	cup finely chopped onions
1/4	pound mushrooms, sliced
1/2	cup pistachio nuts, shelled
1	cup rice
1 1/2	cups chicken stock
	Salt and freshly ground pepper to taste

Sauté onion in margarine until translucent.
Add mushrooms, cook 2 minutes.
Add nuts and rice, stir, add broth and seasonings.
Cover, simmer 17 minutes.

Serves 4

Ruth Gelman

Rice with Pine Nuts and Green Onions

The rice is dressed up with the nutty flavor of pine nuts and green onions and is fabulous with the fresh-tasting parsley.

1/2	cup margarine, divided
2	cups long grain rice
4	cups chicken broth
3/4	cup pine nuts
1	bunch green onions, chopped
1	cup minced fresh parsley
	Salt and fresh ground pepper to taste

Melt 1/4 cup margarine in saucepan.
Add rice and stir until milky, 3 minutes.
Mix in broth, cover, bring to a boil.
Reduce heat, simmer until liquid is absorbed, 20 to 25 minutes.

In another pan, melt remaining margarine.
Add pine nuts, stir until golden brown.
Add green onions and parsley, stir until heated.
Mix into cooked rice, season with salt and pepper.

Serves 12

Marlene Gelman

Hint:
Boiling onions: pour boiling water over sliced onions, let sit 15 minutes, drain and dry them, they'll magically become sweeter.

Risotto Al Funghi

A proper risotto can hardly be made in a hurry. This creamy rice accented with mushrooms and garlic is worth every step. It's to die for!

1 1/2	quarts vegetable broth
2	tablespoons butter or margarine
2	tablespoons olive oil
1	onion, finely chopped
3	garlic cloves, chopped
1/4	cup fresh or frozen porcini mushrooms broken into small pieces, thinly sliced
1/2	cup fresh cremini or portobello mushrooms, thinly sliced
1/2	cup fresh shiitake mushrooms, stems removed, thinly sliced
3	tablespoons chopped fresh parsley, divided
1 1/2	cups white wine
3	cups Arborio rice
3/4	teaspoon salt
1/2	teaspoon pepper
1/2	cup heavy cream or nondairy cream (optional)
3	tablespoons butter (optional)
5	tablespoons grated Parmesan cheese

Bring broth to a boil in a 2 quart covered stockpot, reduce heat, simmer.
In a 4 quart saucepan, cook butter on medium heat, 2 minutes.
Add onion, cook 2 minutes longer.
Reduce heat to low, add garlic, stir well, cook 4 minutes.
Raise heat to medium-high.
Add mushrooms and 1 tablespoon parsley, cook 3 minutes, stirring.
Add wine and deglaze the saucepan, cook 2 minutes.
Add rice, salt and pepper, stir continuously until all wine has evaporated.

Add 3 cups of broth, bring to boil, stirring continuously 2 minutes.
Reduce heat, cover, simmer rice 15 minutes undisturbed.
Stir risotto (it might appear dry).
Raise heat to medium, add 1/2 cup stock, stirring well until incorporated.
Continue adding stock, 1/2 cup at a time, stirring until risotto is cooked (5 to 8 minutes).
(Rice is cooked when tender to the bite.)

Risotto Al Funghi, continued

Turn off heat, add optional cream and butter.
Add remaining parsley, cheese and 1/2 cup remaining simmering stock.
Mix well and let risotto rest for 3 minutes.

*Note: If you cannot find fresh porcini mushroom, you can use dried, about
1/2 to 3/4 ounce. Soften in 2 cups of hot stock about 20 minutes. Chop and
add to other mushrooms. Strain leftover stock into risotto as part of initial
2 cups of liquid.*

Serves 6

Rachel Kalnicki

Risotto Al Ramerino

*Short-grain, Arborio rice is best for making risotto. The grains have a high starch
content that absorbs a lot of liquid without becoming mushy.*

1	**heaping tablespoon rosemary, blanched (fresh or dried)**
1	**clove garlic**
2	**tablespoons margarine**
5	**tablespoons olive oil**
1/2	**cup dry red wine**
2	**cups Arborio rice**
4	**cups vegetable broth**
	Salt and freshly ground pepper to taste

Finely chop rosemary and garlic together.
Heat margarine and oil in casserole over medium heat.
Sauté lightly for 2 minutes.
Add wine, allow to evaporate for 5 minutes.
Add rice, sauté 4 minutes.

Bring broth to a boil in separate saucepan.
Add broth to rice, a small quantity at a time.
Stir gently each time until rice absorbs all broth (16 to 18 minutes).
Season to taste.
Serve immediately, top each serving with fresh ground pepper.

Serves 6

Rachel Kalnicki

Stir-Fried Rice with Cashews

The cooked rice for stir-frying behaves best in the pan when it has been refrigerated, uncovered overnight to dry.

1	cup rice, uncooked
2	tablespoons margarine
2	scallions, finely chopped
10	mushrooms, sliced
2	eggs
1	tablespoon soy sauce
1/4	cup pignoli or cashew nuts, chopped

Cook rice according to package directions, omitting salt, chill.
In a large pan melt margarine, sauté scallions and mushrooms.
Add 2 raw eggs and scramble. Add cooked rice, soy sauce and nuts.

Serves 4

Sophie Goldman

Toasted Barley Casserole

A tasty alternative to rice and a favorite of my son, Michael. Find recipes with oodles of gravy and serve this barley with them. It is a natural sopper-upper!

2	quarts water
1	(8 ounce) package toasted barley
5	tablespoons margarine
1	envelope onion soup mix
1	(4 ounce) can sliced mushrooms, drained

In 2 quarts of boiling water, cook barley 10 minutes, drain.
Add margarine, stir until melted.
Add soup mix and mushrooms, mix.
Pour into a 2 quart ovenproof casserole.
Bake, covered, in a 375 degree oven 30 minutes.
Uncover and bake 10 minutes longer.

Serves 6

Sheila Glasser

148

Gratin of Polenta with Fresh Tomato Sauce and Cheese

In parts of Italy this "Cornmeal Mush" is a staple that often replaces pasta. This is a great accompaniment to chicken.

Polenta:
2 1/2	cups water or light stock
1	cup cornmeal
1	cup cold water
	Salt and freshly ground pepper to taste
	Nutmeg
1/4	cup chopped parsley

Gratin:
2	cups tomato sauce
2	tablespoons butter, melted
1	cup grated Fontina cheese

Polenta:
Bring the water or stock to a boil.
Mix cornmeal with cold water to make a slurry.
Whisk slurry into the boiling liquid.
Continue stirring with a wooden spoon over medium-low heat.
Stir until thick and does not stick to sides of pot.
Season with salt, pepper, nutmeg and parsley.

Pour polenta onto a large wooden board.
Wet hands and evenly smooth polenta to about 1 1/2-inch thick, cool.
Cut cooled polenta into individual servings and continue with gratin.

Spread 1/2-inch layer of tomato sauce in a shallow gratin or baking dish.
Arrange polenta pieces in a single layer.
Brush with melted butter and spoon more tomato sauce lightly on top.
Top with grated cheese, lightly cover with foil.
Heat in 375 degree oven 15 to 20 minutes until hot.
Finish under broiler to brown and melt cheese.

Note: Basic Polenta can be chilled, cut into squares and grilled.

Serves 8

Compliments of Jane Citron

Vegetable Kasha Skillet

A modern interpretation of a traditional eastern European favorite.

1	cup medium kasha
1	egg, beaten
1/4	cup onion, chopped
2	cups water
1	chicken bouillon cube
1 1/2	cups shredded zucchini
1	cup shredded carrots
1/4	cup margarine
	Pepper to taste
	Chopped parsley

Combine kasha, egg and onion.
Cook, stirring constantly until grains are dry and separated.
Add bouillon which has been dissolved in water.
Add vegetables, margarine and pepper, mix well.
Cover, simmer 10 minutes longer, sprinkle with parsley.

Serves 4 to 6

Ruth Gelman

VEGETABLES
VEGETABLES
VEGETABLES

VEGETABLES

Asparagus with Lemon Garlic Vinaigrette

Cooked to tender crispness, this is an all-occasion side dish and the vinaigrette also makes a great salad dressing.

2	cloves garlic
1/2	teaspoon coarse salt
3	tablespoons lemon juice
2	teaspoons Dijon mustard
1/2	teaspoon sugar
3/4	cup olive oil
	Salt and pepper to taste
2	pounds asparagus, tough ends snapped, stems peeled
2	tablespoons fresh flat-leafed parsley, chopped

Using a large knife, mince garlic with the coarse salt.
Scrape garlic into a bowl.
Whisk in lemon juice, mustard and sugar.
Slowly drizzle in olive oil and whisk constantly until thickened.
Season with salt and pepper.

Bring a large skillet of salted water to a boil.
Add asparagus in small batches and cook until crisp tender.
Remove and refresh under cold water.
Drain and dry. Cover and refrigerate.

Just before serving, drizzle with half the vinaigrette.
Sprinkle with parsley. Serve remaining vinaigrette separately.

Serves 6

Ilene Fingeret

Hint:

Roasted asparagus: if roasting potatoes and carrots at the same time, add the asparagus for the last 15 minutes of cooking.

Roasted Asparagus

This is fast, simple, and has a marvelously delicate flavor...with or without the butter.

1 1/2	pounds fresh asparagus, trimmed
2-3	tablespoons extra virgin olive oil
1/4	teaspoon kosher salt, to taste
2	tablespoons unsalted butter, melted (optional)

Spread asparagus on baking sheet, single layer, brush with olive oil.
Sprinkle with salt, place in upper third of oven.
Roast in a 500 degree oven 10 to 12 minutes, until tender.
Pour melted butter over asparagus and serve.

Serves 6

Marlene Gelman

Sweet and Smoky Baked Beans

You don't have to like beans to enjoy this. They're filling, satisfying and slightly sweet. The surprise addition of hot dogs and pastrami make this an indispensable accompaniment to any picnic food or barbecue.

2	small onions, sliced
1	(1 pound) can vegetarian baked beans, drained
1/2	(12 ounce) jar chili sauce
1	tablespoon prepared mustard
1/4	cup molasses
3	tablespoons brown sugar
4-5	hot dogs, cut up
1/4	pound pastrami or beef fry, cut in small pieces

Sauté onions until soft. Combine all ingredients except pastrami.
Pour into a 2 quart casserole, top with pastrami.

Bake, uncovered, in a 250 degree oven 2 1/2 hours.
(If watery, drain some liquid while baking.)
This sauce should be thick. Freezes well.

Serves 4

Dee Selekman

Five Bean Vegetarian Chili

This is great served at an informal party, whether as a vegetarian main course, or as a side dish. Make enough to have plenty of leftovers. For best flavor, cook one day ahead. This freezes beautifully.

3	tablespoons oil
1	tablespoon minced garlic
1	large onion, coarsely chopped
2	large carrots, halved, sliced into 3/4 inch pieces, blanched
1	diced green pepper
1	(16 ounce) can dark red kidney beans, rinsed and drained
1	(16 ounce) can light red kidney beans, rinsed and drained
1	(16 ounce) can black beans, rinsed and drained
1	(16 ounce) can great northern beans, rinsed and drained
1	(8 ounce) can garbanzo beans
1	(28 ounce) can Italian-style tomatoes in puree
1	(28 ounce) can tomato sauce

Heat oil in large soup pot. Add garlic, onions, carrots and green pepper. Sauté until crisp-tender. Add remaining ingredients.
Cover and simmer 45 to 50 minutes, stirring frequently.
May do ahead and freeze.

Note: Do not defrost in microwave, beans get mushy, heat in covered pot.

Serves 6 to 8

Barbara Befferman

Hint:

Three large stalks of cut-up celery added to about two cups of beans (navy, brown, pinto, etc.) will make them more easily digested as will a bit of soda.

Sal's Sicilian Greens and Beans

This is a flavorful Italian dish that will wow guests or family anytime of the year. The beans may be used in any combination, and if you can't find broccoli raab, substitute endive or escarole, it's more common. This is an old world recipe to cherish and pass along. May be used as a side or main dish.

2	**pounds broccoli raab, escarole or endive, washed and trimmed**
3	**tablespoons olive oil**
3-4	**large cloves garlic, minced**
1-2	**(15 1/2 ounce) cans black beans, drained well (or choice of: cannellini beans, garbanzo beans, black-eyed peas)**
1 1/2	**teaspoons salt**
1/2	**teaspoon fresh ground pepper**
1/8	**teaspoon red pepper flakes**

Fill an 8 quart pot with 6 cups of salted water, boil.
Add greens, cook covered, 10 minutes until wilted but not soggy.
Remove, drain well in colander, cool 10 minutes.

Heat olive oil in skillet, sauté garlic 30 seconds.
Add beans, heat; add greens, salt, pepper and red pepper flakes.
Stir gently over med-low heat until hot.
Adjust seasoning and serve immediately.

Serves 4 to 6

Sheila Glasser

Hint:

Broccoli raab: broccoli raab should have long, thin green stalks with crisp dark leaves. A few yellow flowers are fine, but most of the buds should be tightly closed and dark green.

Sephardic Stuffed Cabbage

The rich distinctive flavors of this dish are enticing. Grape leaves may be exchanged for cabbage and can be found in jars or cans in specialty food shops.

1	**small head cabbage**
1/2	**cup rice, uncooked**
1	**teaspoon allspice**
	Pepper to taste
1/4	**cup fresh mint leaves, chopped (or 2 teaspoons dried)**
	Water
2	**teaspoons oil**
1	**tablespoon lemon juice**
1	**clove garlic, minced**

Boil about 20 large cabbage leaves 3 to 5 minutes, until pliable.
Trim thick rib from center of each leaf, leaving 2 halves.
Line bottom of 6 quart pot with remaining ribs and leaves.

In a bowl, mix together rice, allspice, pepper and mint.
Place scant teaspoonful of rice mixture in center of each leaf.
Roll into small, thin cigar shapes, tucking in ends.
Arrange rolls seam side down, on cabbage leaves in pot.

Add oil, lemon juice and garlic, add enough water to barely cover rolls.
Bring to boil, cook covered, 1 hour. Serve as a side dish.

Yields 40 rolls

Audrey Glickman

Matthew and Noah's Favorite Carrots

These delicious carrots cook in no time. Apricots and almonds make this appealing combination extra special.

5	**carrots, peeled, sliced 1/4-inch thick**
2	**teaspoons sugar**
1	**teaspoon brown sugar**
1/2	**teaspoon ground cinnamon**
4	**tablespoons unsalted butter or margarine**
2	**tablespoons fresh orange juice**
	Salt and freshly ground black pepper
10	**dried apricots, slivered**
1/3	**cup sliced almonds, toasted**
1/8	**teaspoon lemon juice**

Cook carrots in water 10 minutes. Rinse under cold water, drain.
Stir sugars and cinnamon together, set aside.

Melt butter in skillet, stir in carrots, orange juice and sugar mixture.
Cook over medium heat until glazed and sauce is slightly thickened (5 minutes).
Season with salt and pepper. Stir in apricots, almonds and lemon juice.
Cook until heated, about 3 minutes. Serve immediately.

Serves 4 to 6

Deborah Fidel

Hint:

A lump of sugar added to water when cooking vegetable greens help retain their color.

Meatless Tzimmes with Pineapple

Tzimmes is a sweetened, baked combination of yams, carrots and dried fruits with or without meat. The flavorful pieces of kishke, along with the pineapple chunks make this compote excellent for a festive holiday dinner. Preparation one or two days in advance improves the flavor.

1	**(20 ounce) can yams, quartered (reserve liquid)**
1	**(16 ounce) can sliced carrots, drained**
1	**(16 ounce) can pineapple chunks (reserve liquid)**
1	**(16 ounce) kishke, sliced in chunks**
	Prunes, dried apricots (optional)
3	**tablespoons honey**
2	**tablespoons brown sugar**

In casserole, place yams, carrots, pineapple and kishke.
Add prunes and dried apricots.
In a sauce pan place 1/2 cup each pineapple and yam juice, honey and brown sugar.

Bring to boil, reduce to 1/2 of original amount. Pour over yam mixture.
Bake uncovered in a 350 degree oven 40 minutes.

Serves 4

Ruth Foreman

Lemon Roasted Cauliflower

This recipe is amazingly effortless and the results are extraordinarily delicious. The roasted cauliflower retains it's fresh-from-the-garden flavor.

1	**head cauliflower, florets**
	Zest and juice of 1/2 lemon
1/4	**cup olive oil**
	Fresh oregano to taste
1	**teaspoon salt**
	Fresh ground pepper to taste

Preheat oven to 450 degrees.
Mix lemon zest, juice, oil, oregano, salt and pepper.
Add cauliflower and toss to coat.

Spread on a baking sheet, roast 20 minutes.
Cauliflower should be soft and evenly brown around edges.

Serves 6

Marlene Gelman

Pearl's Cauliflower Pancakes

A nice alternative to potato pancakes and a great way to serve vegetables to your family. Adding a piece of bread while cauliflower is steaming will eliminate odors.

1	**medium cauliflower, broken into florets**
4	**tablespoons margarine**
2	**onions, chopped**
2	**eggs**
1/2	**cup bread crumbs**
	Salt and pepper to taste
2	**tablespoons chopped parsley**

Steam cauliflower until tender.
Sauté onions in margarine until soft.
Combine all ingredients and mash or process in food processor.

Form into pancakes. Place on greased cookie sheets.
Bake in a 350 degree oven 15 minutes.

Serves 4

Ruth Fauman-Fichman

Corn Fiesta Casserole

This is a more sophisticated dish than corn pudding. There is no better accompaniment for salmon!

1	tablespoon oil
1/2	cup onion, diced
1	cup chopped red bell pepper
1	cup frozen corn
1	(4 ounce) can chopped green chiles
1/4	teaspoon cumin
1/2	teaspoon chili powder
2	tablespoons butter
1	tablespoon whole wheat flour
2	cups 2% or skim milk
1	cup yellow cornmeal
1 1/2	cups grated cheese, divided

Sauté onion, red pepper and corn in oil until tender.
Stir in chili peppers and spices.

In medium-sized saucepan melt butter, stir in flour.
Slowly add milk and cornmeal. Stir until thick, about 5 minutes.
Mix in the vegetables and 1 cup of cheese.

Pour into a 8-inch square baking dish.
Sprinkle with remaining 1/2 cup of cheese.
Bake in a 350 degree oven 40 to 45 minutes.

Serves 6

Marianne Silberman

Hint:
Corn: when boiling corn, add sugar to water instead of salt. Salt with toughen corn.

Blue Cheese Baked Mushrooms

When you get tired of serving potatoes, switch to this mushroom casserole. It probably has the same number of calories, but it's so good!

2	**pounds large fresh mushrooms**
1/2	**cup crumbled blue cheese (about 3 ounces)**
1	**cup dry bread crumbs**
1/8	**teaspoon chives, minced**
2	**tablespoons butter**
1/4	**cup sherry**
1/2	**cup heavy cream**

Remove stems from mushrooms.
Place a small piece of blue cheese in cavity of each mushroom.
Sauté bread crumbs and chives in butter.
Toss crumbs with remaining blue cheese.

Layer half of the crumbs in 8 x 11-inch buttered casserole.
Place mushrooms, cavity side up, on crumbs. Drizzle wine over top.
Sprinkle with remaining half of cheese crumbs.
Pour cream carefully over mixture.
Bake, covered, in a 375 degree oven 25 minutes.

Serves 6

Reva Nieman

Red Onion Pickles

Onions that are tenderly dressed with anchovies, oil and vinegar.

1	**pound red onions, peeled**
1 1/3	**cups red wine vinegar**
1/2	**cup sherry wine vinegar**
1 1/2	**tablespoons sugar**
1	**cup water**
2	**bay leaves**
4	**anchovy fillets, finely chopped**
1	**tablespoon finely chopped parsley**
3	**tablespoons olive oil**
	Freshly ground pepper to taste

Cut the onions into wedges, separate layers.
In saucepan, combine vinegars, sugar, water and bay leaves.
Add onion slices, cover with liquid.
Bring to boil, cook 4 minutes over medium high heat.
Stir onions often to assure even cooking.

Strain onions, discard liquid, cool.
Combine anchovies, parsley, pepper and oil.
Blend well and pour over onions.
Refrigerate overnight. Serve chilled.

Serves 10

Elaine Beck

Hint:

Leeks: leeks are milder and sweeter than onions. Use white portion only, washed well.

Snow Peas Oriental

This recipe will bring you nothing but compliments and requests for more.

1	teaspoon light sesame oil
1/2	pound fresh snow pea pods, trimmed
1/2	cup carrots, diagonally sliced thin
1/4	cup sliced water chestnuts
1/2	cup chicken broth
1	teaspoon low sodium soy sauce
1	teaspoon cornstarch

Coat a nonstick skillet with cooking spray.
Add oil, place over medium high heat until hot.
Add snow peas and carrots, sauté 2 minutes.
Add water chestnuts and broth, bring to a boil.
Cover, reduce heat and simmer 5 minutes or until crisp-tender.

Combine soy sauce and cornstarch, stir until dissolved.
Add to vegetable mixture.
Cook over medium heat until sauce thickens. Serve immediately.

Serves 4

Sheila Cohen

Oriental Spinach with Ginger and Garlic

My family never liked spinach until I served it this way. Stir frying preserves the fresh flavor and texture of vegetables being cooked.

1	(10 ounce) bag fresh spinach, washed, drained well
2	teaspoons olive oil
1	teaspoon fresh ginger, minced
1	clove garlic, minced
2	scallions, chopped
	Salt and pepper to taste

Heat oil in large skillet or wok.
Stir fry ginger and garlic until fragrant (10 to 15 seconds).
Add scallions, stir fry 1 minute.
Add spinach, stir fry until wilted (about 1 minute).
Season spinach with salt and pepper. Serve immediately.

Serves 3

Sheila Glasser

Spinach and Cheese in Phyllo Pastry

The phyllo pastry is buttery, flaky, golden brown, and dresses up this delicious dish.

3	**(10 ounce) packages frozen chopped spinach**
2	**(10 1/2 ounce) cans cream of mushroom soup, undiluted**
4	**eggs, beaten**
	Salt and pepper to taste
3	**cups grated mozzarella cheese**
1	**(1 pound) package phyllo dough**
3/4	**cup butter or margarine, melted**

Defrost spinach, drain, squeeze out all moisture.
Butter bottom of 13 x 9-inch baking dish.
Combine spinach, soup, eggs, salt and pepper in a bowl.
Layer 5 sheets phyllo in bottom of pan, butter top of each sheet.

Spread 1/2 of spinach mixture over first layer of phyllo.
Top with 2 buttered sheets phyllo. Spread with 1/2 the cheese.
Repeat layering with remaining spinach and cheese.
End with 2 buttered sheets phyllo (may be frozen at this point).
Bake covered in a 350 degree oven 50 minutes.

Note: To cook after frozen, bring to room temperature, top with melted butter, then bake.

Serves 10 to 12

Annette Barnett

Skillet Barbecued Tofu

A great vegetarian meal. An earthly blend of aromas and flavors.

1/2	cup soy sauce
3	tablespoons honey (or rice syrup)
2	tablespoons canola (or sesame oil)
2	teaspoons dry mustard
2	teaspoons onion powder
4	garlic cloves minced (or 1/2 teaspoon garlic powder)
	Oil for frying
1 1/2	pounds firm tofu, sliced
	Chopped scallions (garnish)
	Cooked rice

Combine all ingredients except tofu, scallions and rice, mix.
Add tofu and marinate refrigerated (not more than 2 hours).

Heat oil in skillet, brown tofu slices on both sides.
Garnish with scallions and serve hot over rice.

Serves 4

Lisa Katz

Fruit Stuffed Acorn Squash

The slightly sweet flavor of this delicious squash with a spoonful of brown sugar, a little liqueur and some pecans baked in the middle, combined with fruit, seem to appeal to young and old alike.

1	acorn squash, halved (seeds and fibers removed)
1	tablespoon butter
4	tablespoons yellow raisins
2	tablespoons Galliano liqueur
2	tablespoons pecans, chopped and toasted
2	tablespoons brown sugar

Butter outside of squash. Arrange cut side down on cookie sheet.
Bake in a 350 degree oven for 20 to 30 minutes.

Soak yellow raisins in Galliano 25 minutes.
When squash is soft, turn over.
Fill with raisins, pecans and brown sugar, broil 5 minutes.

Serves 2 to 4

Myra Judd

Zucchini Feta Casserole

An impressive dish that is delicious and suitable for company. This raises the casserole from the ordinary to the extraordinary.

3/4	cup bulgur wheat
1/4	cup boiling water
2 1/2	tablespoons vegetable oil
2	cups sliced onions
4	cloves garlic, minced
6	cups thinly sliced zucchini
1/2	teaspoon dried oregano
1/2	teaspoon dried basil
1/2	teaspoon dried marjoram
1/8	teaspoon black pepper
2	eggs
1	cup feta cheese
1	cup cottage cheese
1/2-1	cup chopped fresh parsley
2	tablespoons tomato paste
1	tablespoon tamari soy sauce
1	cup grated Cheddar cheese
2	medium tomatoes, thinly sliced
1-1 1/2	tablespoons sesame seeds (optional)

Place bulgur in bowl, cover with boiling water.
Cover, set aside until water is absorbed and bulgur is soft and chewable.
Sauté onions and garlic in oil until translucent.
Add zucchini, dried herbs and black pepper.
Sauté on medium to low heat until zucchini is tender.

In a bowl lightly beat eggs. Mix in feta and cottage cheese.
Add parsley, tomato paste and soy sauce to bulgur, mix well.
Grease 9 x 9-inch casserole dish.
Layer in order, bulgur mixture, sautéed vegetables and feta mixture.
Top with Cheddar cheese and tomatoes.
End with a light sprinkling of sesame seeds.

Bake covered in a 350 degree oven 45 minutes.
(For crustier topping, uncover casserole for final 15 minutes of baking.)
Allow to sit 5 to 10 minutes before serving. Serve with tossed salad.

Serves 6

Ilene Fingeret

Layered Roasted Vegetables with Tomato Sauce and Mozzarella Cheese

Delicious and colorful. This is an outstanding vegetable casserole to accompany almost any main dish.

1/3	cup minced fresh parsley
1 1/2	tablespoons grated Parmesan cheese
1/4	teaspoon salt
1	clove garlic, minced
1/2	pound small round red potatoes, thinly sliced
1	cup sliced zucchini
1	cup sliced yellow squash
1	cup sliced fresh mushrooms
1/2	cup chopped leeks
2	(8 ounce) cans tomato sauce
1/4	cup shredded mozzarella cheese

Combine first 4 ingredients in a small bowl, stir well.
Coat a 11 x 7-inch baking dish or casserole with nonstick cooking spray.
Place layer of potatoes on bottom.
Layer with zucchini, squash and mushrooms.
Sprinkle with 1/4 of parsley mixture over each layer. Top with leeks.

Pour tomato sauce over layered vegetables. Cover with aluminum foil and vent.
Bake in a 350 degree oven 45 minutes.
Uncover, sprinkle with mozzarella cheese.
Bake uncovered 5 minutes longer or until cheese melts.

Serves 6

Florie Krell

DESSERTS

DESSERTS

CAKES

PIES

COOKIES AND BARS

OTHER DESSERTS

Applesauce Nut Cake with Dates and Raisins

A little tinkering can turn a homemade cake into an incredible taste sensation.

1/2	cup margarine
1	cup sugar
1	egg, beaten
1	teaspoon vanilla
2	cups flour
2	teaspoons baking soda
1	cup dates, sliced
1 1/2	cups applesauce
1	cup coarsely chopped nuts
1	cup raisins, chopped
1/2	teaspoon cinnamon
1/4	teaspoon ground cloves

Preheat oven to 350 degrees.
Cream margarine and sugar, add egg and vanilla.
Add rest of ingredients in order given. Blend well.
Bake in a well greased 9 x 5-inch loaf pan, 1 hour.

Serves 8

Thea Bernstein

Hint:
For baking, it's best to use medium to large eggs. Extra large may cause cakes to fall when cooked.

Best Blueberry Cake

There is something wonderfully light and summery about this quick cake that takes advantage of fresh blueberries.

2	cups sugar
1	cup margarine
4	eggs, at room temperature
1/2	teaspoon salt
1	teaspoon vanilla
3	cups flour
2	cups blueberries (1 pint)

Cream sugar and margarine until well combined.
Beat in eggs, one at a time.
Add salt, vanilla and flour, mix well.
Gently fold in well drained blueberries.
Grease a 13 x 9-inch pan. Bake in 350 degree oven 1 hour.

Serves 12

Sally Samuels

Hint:
Slicing cake: use dental floss to slice evenly and cleanly through a cake or torte. Simply stretch a length of the floss taut and press down through the cake.

Blueberry Pound Cake with Almonds

A beautiful cake for a festive occasion. If you like blueberries, this one is just right.

3/4	**cup unsalted butter, room temperature**
2	**cups sugar**
3	**large eggs**
3	**cups flour**
1	**tablespoon baking powder**
1/2	**teaspoon salt**
3/4	**cup whole milk**
1 1/2	**cups blueberries (tossed with 1 tablespoon flour)**
1	**cup toasted slivered almonds**
	Powdered sugar (for dusting)
	Additional blueberries

Preheat oven to 350 degrees.
Spray a 12 cup Bundt pan with nonstick spray.
In large bowl, cream butter and sugar together with electric mixer.
Add eggs, one at a time, beating well after each addition (mixture will be firm).

In another bowl, combine flour, baking powder and salt.
Gradually add to butter mixture, alternating with milk.
Add blueberries that have been tossed with flour, using a rubber spatula.
Pour batter into prepared pan, sprinkle almonds evenly over batter.

Bake in center of oven 1 hour 15 minutes or until a toothpick inserted comes out clean.
Cool cake in pan, about 20 minutes.
Unmold carefully onto cake rack, cool completely.

To serve:
Carefully transfer cake to serving dish, dust with powdered sugar.
Fill center with additional blueberries.

Serves 16

Compliments of Rania Harris
Rania's Catering

Brazilian Chocolate Cake

This appealing cake is a natural for your most elegant gatherings.

3	**cups flour**
2	**cups sugar**
1	**cup cocoa powder**
1	**teaspoon baking powder**
1	**teaspoon baking soda**
1/2	**teaspoon salt**
2	**eggs**
1	**cup oil**
2	**cups boiling water**

Glaze:

1/2	**cup sugar**
2	**tablespoons cocoa powder**
2	**tablespoons margarine**
3	**tablespoons water**

In a bowl, add all dry ingredients for cake.
Add eggs and oil, stir with a wooden spoon.
Add boiling water, mix well.

Pour mixture into a well greased, lightly floured 9 x 13-inch baking pan.
Bake in 350 degree oven 30 minutes or until a toothpick inserted comes out clean.
Slowly melt glaze ingredients in a sauce pan. Drizzle over cake when cool.

Serves 12

Rachel Kalnicki

Caramelized Banana Walnut Upside Down Cake

This great tasting cake has a gooey caramel topping loaded with walnuts.

Topping:

1	cup packed light brown sugar
1/4	cup unsalted margarine
3	tablespoons pure maple syrup
1/4	cup walnuts, coarsely chopped and toasted
4	large ripe bananas cut diagonally into 1/4-inch slices

Cake:

1	cup flour
2	teaspoons baking powder
1/2	teaspoon cinnamon
1/4	teaspoon salt
3/4	cup sugar
6	tablespoons unsalted margarine (room temperature)
1	large egg
1/2	teaspoon vanilla
6	tablespoons nondairy creamer

Topping:
Stir sugar and margarine in saucepan over low heat until melted and well blended.
Pour into a 9-inch cake pan with 2-inch high sides. Spread to coat bottom of pan.
Pour maple syrup over sugar mixture, sprinkle nuts.
Place banana slices in circular design on nuts, overlapping slightly, covering bottom.

Preheat oven to 325 degrees.
Stir flour, baking powder, cinnamon and salt in bowl, set aside.
Beat sugar and butter in mixing bowl until creamy.
Add egg and vanilla, beat until light and fluffy.
Beat in flour mixture alternately with creamer in 3 additions.
Spoon batter over bananas.
Bake 55 minutes or until toothpick inserted into center of cake comes out clean.

Run knife around pan sides. Cool cake on rack 30 minutes.
Place plate over pan, invert cake. Let stand 3 minutes, then gently lift off pan.

Serve 8 to 10

Harriet Kruman

Chocolate Covered Marble Cheesecake

Everyone loves a happy ending. This knockout dessert can be the main attraction of any dinner, luncheon, or buffet.

Crust:

1 1/2	cups finely crushed vanilla wafers
6	tablespoons butter or margarine, melted

Filling:

2	(8 ounce) packages cream cheese, softened
1	cup cheese (see Note)
1	teaspoon orange zest
1	teaspoon vanilla
1	cup sugar
2	tablespoons flour
1/2	teaspoon salt
2	eggs
1	egg yolk
1/2	cup milk
2	ounces semisweet chocolate, melted

Topping:

6	ounces semisweet chocolate
2	tablespoons shortening
1	orange, peeled, sliced and cut in half
	Shredded orange zest (garnish)

Prepare crust: stir together crushed wafers and melted butter.
Press firmly on bottom and 1 3/4-inch up sides of 8-inch springform pan.

Beat cream cheese and desired cheese until creamy.
Add orange peel (omit if desired cheese has orange in it) and vanilla.
Combine sugar, flour and salt in separate bowl, gradually blend into cheese mixture.
Add eggs and egg yolk all at once, beat just until blended. Stir in milk.

Pour 1/2 (about 2 cups) of mixture into another bowl.
To remaining filling, add chocolate, stir well. Alternate fillings into pan.
Using narrow spatula, stir gently through batter for a marbled effect.

Chocolate Covered Marble Cheesecake, continued

Bake in a 450 degree oven 10 minutes.
Reduce heat to 300 degrees, bake approximately 40 minutes longer, until center appears set.
Remove from oven, cool 15 minutes. Loosen sides, cool 30 minutes more.
Remove sides of pan. Cover and chill 2 hours.

Prepare topping:
Melt chocolate and shortening over low heat, spread over chilled cake.
Chill again until set. Garnish with ring of orange slices and orange zest.

Note: Cheese options: Drained cottage cheese, cream cheese, Danish orange cream cheese, orange or walnut-flavored Gourmandise, Neufchâtel, or ricotta.

Serves 12

Dee Selekman

Chocolate Chip Vinegar Cake

This cake is so wonderful, it's hard to stop eating!

1 2/3	**cups flour**
1	**cup light brown sugar, packed**
1/4	**cup cocoa**
1	**teaspoon baking soda**
1	**cup water**
1/3	**cup oil**
3/4	**teaspoon vanilla extract**
1	**teaspoon vinegar**
1/2	**cup chocolate chips**

In small bowl, combine flour, sugar, cocoa and baking soda.
Add water, oil, vanilla and vinegar, beat until smooth.

Pour batter into greased and lightly floured 8 x 8-inch pan.
Sprinkle with chocolate chips.
Bake in 350 degree oven 35 to 40 minutes or until inserted toothpick comes out clean.
Cool in pan on wire rack.

Serves 8

Edy Baron

Chocolate, Chocolate Chip Banana Cake

Here's an easy way to use a stray ripe banana. This cake goes together in a jiffy.

1/2	cup butter
1	cup sugar
2	eggs
1/2	cup sour cream
1	large banana, mashed
1	teaspoon vanilla
1 1/2	cups flour
6	tablespoons cocoa
1	teaspoon baking powder
1/2	teaspoon baking soda
2	cups mini morsel chocolate chips
	Powdered sugar

Cream butter and sugar, beat in eggs.
Beat in sour cream, banana and vanilla, stir until blended.
Add remaining ingredients, blend well (do not over beat).

Spread batter in greased 10-inch tube pan.
Bake in 350 degree oven 40 to 45 minutes, until toothpick inserted comes out clean.
Cool in pan, remove, sprinkle with powdered sugar.

Serves 10

Thea Bernstein

Hint:

Bananas: the ripest bananas make the best banana bread. Overripe bananas, peeled first, freeze very well so you can collect them and make this bread when you need it.

Chocolate Chunk Sour Cream Cake

This is a sophisticated, rich cake that's great for brunch, lunch, or any time.

Filling:

1/4	cup sugar
2	teaspoons cinnamon
12	ounces semisweet chocolate, coarsely chopped
1	cup coarsely chopped walnuts

Cake:

2 3/4	cups flour
2	teaspoons baking powder
1/2	teaspoon baking soda
1	cup unsalted butter, softened
1	cup sugar
3	eggs
1 1/2	teaspoons vanilla
1	cup sour cream

In a small bowl, combine sugar and cinnamon.
Add chocolate and walnuts, stir. Set filling aside.

Preheat oven to 350 degrees.
In a medium bowl, mix flour, baking powder and baking soda.
In a large bowl, beat butter until creamy.
Gradually add sugar, beat until light and fluffy.
Add eggs, one at a time, beating well after each addition.
Add vanilla. Add dry ingredients alternately with sour cream.

Spread 1/3 of batter in greased and lightly floured 10-inch tube pan.
Cover batter with 1/3 of filling.
Repeat two more times ending with filling on top.

Bake 55 to 65 minutes until toothpick inserted in center is clean.
Cool cake on a wire rack for 15 minutes, until chocolate on top starts to harden.
Run a knife around edge of pan to loosen, invert onto a wire rack.
Invert onto another wire rack and cool completely.

Serves 12

Marlene Gelman

Cranberry Streusel Coffee Cake

This cranberry creation is a favorite at our house and a showstopper on a brunch table. It's a sweet coffee cake that makes great eating any time of the day.

Streusel:

3/4	cup pecans, chopped
2/3	cup light brown sugar, packed
1/4	cup butter or margarine, softened
1	tablespoon ground cinnamon

1 3/4	cups sugar
3/4	cup butter or margarine, softened
2	teaspoons baking powder
2	teaspoons baking soda
1	teaspoon salt
1	tablespoon vanilla extract
4	large eggs
1 1/2	cups dried cranberries (7 1/2 ounces)
4	cups flour
2	cups sour cream

Preheat oven to 350 degrees. Spray a 10-inch tube pan with nonstick spray. Combine streusel ingredients with a fork until blended, set aside.

Using electric mixer combine sugar, butter, baking powder, soda and salt. Beat 5 minutes on high until fluffy.
Reduce to medium speed, beat in vanilla, add eggs one at a time to blend. Stir in cranberries.
Alternately, stir in flour and sour cream in 3 additions until blended.

Pour 5 cups batter in prepared pan, smooth top.
Scatter 3/4 cup of streusel mix over the batter.
Repeat layers with remaining batter and streusel.
Bake 1 hour or until top is golden and a toothpick comes out clean.
Cool completely before lifting out of pan.

Serves 10 to 12

Judy Papernick

Cranberry Swirl Coffee Cake

This recipe may not be the best in the whole world, but it comes fairly close.

1	cup sugar
1/2	cup margarine
2	eggs
1	teaspoon vanilla
2	cups flour
1	teaspoon baking powder
1	teaspoon baking soda
1/2	teaspoon salt
8	ounces sour cream
1	(8 ounce) can whole cranberry sauce
1/2	cup chopped nuts

Cream sugar and margarine. Add eggs, one at a time, add vanilla.
Add dry ingredients, alternately with sour cream.

Pour 1/2 of batter into 8-inch tube pan, then 1/2 of cranberry sauce.
Add remaining batter.
Spoon remaining cranberry sauce on top, cover with chopped nuts.
Bake in 350 degree oven 50 minutes.

Serves 10 to 12

Marlene Gelman

Honey Cocoa Cake

One bite is all it takes to figure out why this recipe is so special.

3/4	cup honey
1	cup sugar
2	eggs
1	teaspoon cinnamon
1	teaspoon baking powder
1	teaspoon baking soda
2	cups sifted flour
1	teaspoon cocoa
1/2	cup plus 1 tablespoon oil
1	cup cold coffee
1	cup chopped nuts

Blend honey and sugar, add eggs, beat.
Sift dry ingredients, add to honey mixture alternating with oil.
Carefully blend in coffee, add nuts (mixture will be very thin).
Pour into ungreased 9 x 5-loaf pan.
Bake in a 350 degree oven 1 hour 15 minutes.

Serves 8 to 10

Ruth Lasday

Hint:

Measure Sticky Liquid: before measuring honey or syrup, oil the cup with cooking oil and rinse in hot water.

Lemon Pound Cake

A wonderful cake for lemon lovers like me - lemony, buttery, and moist.

1	**cup margarine**
2 3/4	**cups sugar**
6	**eggs**
3	**cups flour**
1/2	**teaspoon salt**
1/4	**teaspoon baking powder**
1	**cup lemon yogurt**
1/2	**teaspoon vanilla**
1/2	**teaspoon grated lemon peel**
1/2	**cup chopped walnuts**

Beat margarine until fluffy. Add sugar, beat about 15 minutes.
Add eggs one at a time.
In a bowl, combine flour, salt and baking powder.
In separate bowl, combine yogurt, lemon peel and vanilla.

Add flour and yogurt mixtures gradually, beginning and ending with flour mixture.
Stir in nuts. Bake in preheated 325 degree oven 1 hour, 20 minutes.

Note: May prepare in cupcake tins, large baking pan or loaf pans.

Serves 12

Judy Papernick

My Mother's Moist Fruit Cake

This raisin-studded creation features plenty of citrus flavor as well as the crunchy taste of walnuts.

1	cup raisins
1	cup water
2	teaspoons baking soda
1	cup unsalted margarine or shortening
2	cups sugar
4	jumbo eggs
1	teaspoon vanilla
4	cups sifted flour
2	teaspoons baking powder
2	cups crushed pineapple, with juice
1	cup coarsely chopped walnuts

Preheat oven to 325 degrees.
Bring raisins, water and baking soda to a boil, set aside to cool.
Cream margarine with sugar, add eggs, mix well.
Add vanilla, fold in raisins and liquid.

Sift flour and baking soda together 3 times, fold into sugar mixture.
Fold in pineapple, nuts and stir.
Pour into a greased and floured 9 x 13-inch pan.
Bake 1 hour or until a toothpick inserted comes out dry.

Serves 12

Margie Herer

Pareve Chocolate Layer Cake

A delicious chocolate cake with chocolate frosting that is perfect after a meat dinner.

3/4	cup margarine
1 3/4	cups sugar
2	eggs
1	teaspoon vanilla
2	cups flour
3/4	cup cocoa
1 1/4	teaspoons baking soda
1/2	teaspoon salt
1 1/3	cups water

Frosting:

6	ounces unsweetened chocolate, melted
1 1/2	cups powdered sugar
3	tablespoons hot water
3	pasteurized eggs (or egg substitute)
1/2	cup margarine, softened

Cream margarine and sugar until light and fluffy.
Add eggs and vanilla, beat 1 minute at medium speed.
Combine flour, cocoa, baking soda and salt.
Add alternately with water to creamed mixture.

Pour batter into 2 greased and floured 8-inch cake pans.
Bake in 350 degree oven 35 to 40 minutes. Cool.

Frosting:
With mixer at low speed, beat chocolate, sugar and water until blended.
Add eggs one at a time, beating well after each addition.
Add margarine, beat until smooth. Spread on cool cake.

Serves 12

Barbara Befferman

Pumpkin Cake with Chocolate Chips

People's eyes roll when they take their first bite!

4	eggs
2	cups sugar
1	cup oil
1	(16 ounce) can pumpkin
3	cups flour
2	teaspoons baking powder
2	teaspoons baking soda
1/2	teaspoon salt
1/2	teaspoon cinnamon
6	ounces chocolate chips

Preheat oven to 400 degrees.
Beat eggs with sugar. Add oil and pumpkin.
Add dry ingredients, mix well. Stir in chocolate chips.

Pour batter into a Bundt pan coated with nonstick spray.
Reduce heat, bake in 350 degree oven 1 hour 10 minutes.
Cool in pan.

Serves 12

Ilene Fingeret

Purple Plum Torte

This beautiful dessert is the perfect choice for a special dinner party.

1	**cup sugar**
1/2	**cup unsalted butter or margarine**
1	**cup unbleached flour, sifted**
1	**teaspoon baking powder**
1/2	**teaspoon salt**
2	**eggs**
12	**purple plums, halved and pitted**
2	**teaspoons sugar**
2	**teaspoons lemon juice**
2	**teaspoons cinnamon**

Cream sugar and butter until light.
Add flour, baking powder, salt and eggs.
Spoon the batter into a 9-inch springform pan.
Cover the top with plums, skin side up.

Sprinkle lightly with sugar and lemon juice.
Sprinkle with cinnamon. Bake in 350 degree oven 1 hour.

Serve warm, plain or with ice cream or whipped cream.
May be refrigerated or frozen.

Note: Any fruit/nut combination may be used: apples and walnuts; bananas and almonds.

Serves 12

Rachel Kalnicki

Streusel Cake A L'Orange

This has an enticing hint of orange, looks sophisticated, tastes terrific.

Streusel:

1	cup light brown sugar
1	cup chopped walnuts
1/4	cup flour
3	tablespoons melted butter
1	teaspoon grated orange zest

Cake:

1/2	cup butter or margarine, softened
1/2	cup granulated sugar
3	large eggs
1	teaspoon grated orange zest
1/2	teaspoon vanilla
2	cups flour
1	teaspoon baking powder
1	teaspoon baking soda
2/3	cup orange juice

Glaze:

1/2	cup powdered sugar
2 1/2	teaspoons orange juice

Streusel:
Combine brown sugar, nuts and flour. Stir in butter and orange zest, set aside.

Cake:
Preheat oven to 350 degrees.
With electric mixer on medium speed, mix butter and sugar together until fluffy.
Add eggs one at a time, beat well. Add orange zest and vanilla.

Mix flour, baking powder and baking soda together in separate bowl.
Beat in flour mixture alternately with orange juice, beginning and ending with flour.

Pour 1/2 of batter into greased 9 or 10-inch tube baking pan.
Sprinkle with 1/2 of the streusel. Top with remaining batter and streusel.
Bake 45 minutes or until a toothpick comes out clean. Cool completely.

Streusel Cake A L'Orange, continued

Glaze:
Stir together sugar and orange juice, drizzle on top of cake.

Serves 12 to 14

Charilee Levy

Unbeatable Zucchini Loaf Cake

This absolutely exceptional cake is my most famous recipe.

3	**eggs**
2	**cups sugar**
1	**cup vegetable oil**
2 1/2	**cups flour**
2	**teaspoons baking soda**
1	**teaspoon baking powder**
1	**teaspoon salt**
3	**teaspoons cinnamon**
2	**cups grated zucchini, unpeeled**
2	**teaspoons vanilla**
1	**cup chopped walnuts**

Beat eggs lightly.
Beat in sugar gradually, then oil, mix well.
Mix flour with baking soda, baking powder, salt and cinnamon.
Add to egg mixture alternately with zucchini.
Stir in vanilla and walnuts, mix well.

Pour into 2 greased and lightly floured 9 x 5-inch loaf pans.
Bake in 350 degree oven 45 to 50 minutes.
Cool for about 10 minutes, remove from pans.

Yields 2 loaves

Bunny Morris

Walnut Honey Cake

Guaranteed to win new honey cake devotees.

6	eggs, separated
1 1/2	cups sugar
1	pound honey
1	cup oil
1	cup black coffee
1	teaspoon vanilla
3 1/2	cups flour
1/2	teaspoon salt
1/2	teaspoon cinnamon
1	teaspoon baking powder
1	teaspoon baking soda
1	cup chopped walnuts

Beat yolks with sugar until light and thick
Add honey, beat thoroughly.
Add oil, coffee and vanilla alternately with dry ingredients.

Fold in stiffly beaten egg whites. Add nuts.
Pour into a large ungreased angel food cake pan.
Bake in a 350 degree oven 1 hour.

Serves 12

Ruth Lasday

Hint:

Cupcakes: an ice cream scoop can be used to fill cupcake papers without spilling.

Zucchini Carrot Cake with Cream Cheese Frosting

An easy, make-ahead cake for those with a sweet tooth.

2	**eggs**
1	**cup sugar**
2/3	**cup canola oil**
1 1/4	**cups flour**
1	**teaspoon baking soda**
1	**teaspoon baking powder**
1	**teaspoon cinnamon**
1	**cup grated zucchini**
1	**cup grated carrots**
1/2	**cup chopped nuts**
2	**ounces cream cheese**
2	**tablespoons margarine**
1 2/3	**cups powdered sugar**
1	**teaspoon vanilla**

Beat eggs and sugar until frothy, gradually beat in oil.
Add dry ingredients, beat at high speed 4 minutes.
Stir in zucchini, carrots and nuts.

Pour into 9-inch square baking dish coated with nonstick spray.
Bake in 350 degree oven 35 minutes or until top springs back when touched. Cool.

In small bowl, blend cream cheese and margarine.
Add sugar and vanilla, beat until smooth. Spread on cool cake.

Serves 8 to 10

Edy Baron

Any Fresh Fruit Pie

Mix or match fresh fruit when it is plentiful for a summer treat. Serve hot or cold.

2	pints berries (strawberries, blueberries, etc.), divided
1	cup water, divided
1	cup sugar (more or less depending on berry sweetness)
1	tablespoon lemon juice
3	tablespoons cornstarch
1	9-inch baked pie shell
	Whipped cream for topping (optional)

Place 1 pint of berries, 1/2 cup of water, sugar and lemon juice into sauce pan.
Bring to a rolling boil.
Dissolve cornstarch in a scant 1/2 cup water.
Add to the berry mixture, stir until thickened.

Add second pint of berries, cool.
Pour into baked shell.
Entire pie or individual slices may be topped with whipped cream.

Serves 6 to 8

Beverly Robins

Bourbon Chocolate Nut Pie

This incredibly easy to prepare pie is a showstopper!

2	eggs
1	cup sugar
1/2	cup margarine, melted
3/4	tablespoon bourbon
1/4	cup cornstarch
1	cup nuts, chopped
1	cup chocolate chips
1	(9 inch) pie crust, unbaked

Mix all ingredients together, pour into pie shell.
Bake in a 350 degree oven 40 to 45 minutes.
Cool on wire rack.

Serves 8

Lisa Steindel

Apple Walnut Cream Cheese Pie with Caramel Topping

Give this pie a try - it's terrific. Guaranteed to ruin your teeth and your figure!

4	**large apples, cored and sliced**
2	**teaspoons cinnamon**
1	**teaspoon lemon juice**
1	**10-inch pie crust, unbaked**
2	**(8 ounce) packages cream cheese**
2	**tablespoons sour cream**
1	**teaspoon cornstarch**
1	**teaspoon vanilla**
2	**eggs**

Topping:

2	**cups light or dark brown sugar**
3	**tablespoons butter, melted**
1/2	**cup chopped walnuts**

Toss apples with cinnamon and lemon juice.
Place in a 10-inch pie crust.
In blender, combine cream cheese, sour cream, cornstarch, vanilla and eggs.
Pour this mixture over apples in crust.

Mix topping ingredients. Sprinkle over pie, pat down.
Cover with foil, bake in 350 degrees 45 minutes.
Remove foil, bake 15 minutes longer. Serve cold.

Serves 8

Marlene Gelman

Dutch Chocolate Mousse Pie

Decadence for a chocoholic! Worth every calorie.

Crust:

1 1/4	cups fine graham cracker crumbs
1/4	cup sugar
6	tablespoons margarine, melted

Filling:

8	ounces semisweet chocolate (or 8 ounces of semisweet chocolate chips)
4	tablespoons water
8	pasteurized eggs, separated
1	teaspoon vanilla
2/3	cup sugar

Crust:
Combine graham cracker crumbs, sugar and margarine.
Press mixture firmly into 9-inch pie pan.
Bake in a 375 degree oven 6 to 8 minutes or until edges are browned.
Cool.

Filling:
Melt chocolate with water over very low heat, stirring until smooth.
Stir in egg yolks, add vanilla.
Beat egg whites in mixing bowl until foamy.
Gradually add sugar, continue beating until stiff peaks form.
Stir small amount egg whites into chocolate mixture.
Fold chocolate mixture into remaining meringue mixture.
Pour filling into crust. Chill at least 3 hours before serving.

Note: Eggs separate easier at room temperature.

Serves 6

Reva Neiman

Pecan Pie with Kahlúa and Chocolate Chips

This pie is wickedly gooey, sinfully rich, and simple to prepare.

1/2	cup sugar
1/4	cup unsalted butter, room temperature
1	tablespoon all purpose flour
3/4	cup dark corn syrup
1/4	cup Kahlúa
1	teaspoon vanilla extract
3	large eggs
1	cup pecans, chopped
1/2	cup semisweet chocolate chips
1	prepared frozen deep dish 9-inch pie crust
1	cup chilled whipping cream
	Toasted pecan halves (garnish)

Preheat oven to 375 degrees.
Beat sugar and butter in medium bowl until smooth. Add flour.
Gradually beat in corn syrup, Kahlúa and vanilla.
Mix in eggs, then chopped pecans.

Sprinkle chocolate chips over bottom of crust. Pour filling into crust.
Bake about 45 minutes until filling is puffed around edges and just set in the center.
(Cover edge of crust with foil if browning too quickly.)
Transfer pie to cooling rack, cool completely.

Beat cream in medium bowl until peaks form.
Drop whipped cream in small dollops around edge of pie or pipe a decorative edge using a pastry bag fitted with a star tip.
Place pecan halves on top of the whipped cream border.

Serves 8

Compliments of Rania Harris
Rania's Catering

Southern Sweet Potato Pie

I prefer the delicate flavor of this creamy pie to the more traditional pumpkin pie. I thank my friend Zetra Rose for this wonderful recipe.

4	(9 inch) deep-dish pie crusts, baked
2	(40 ounce) cans yams, drained
4	eggs, beaten
2 1/2	cups sugar
2	teaspoons cinnamon
1	teaspoon nutmeg
1	teaspoon lemon extract
2	teaspoons vanilla
2	(14 ounce) cans evaporated milk
	Nondairy whipped topping

Combine all ingredients in large bowl, blend until smooth.
Pour filling into crusts and place on baking sheet.
Bake in a 400 degree oven 15 minutes.
Reduce heat to 350, bake 40 to 50 minutes longer. Cool on rack.
Serve with nondairy whipped topping. Freezes very well.

Yields 4 pies

Sheila Glasser

Hint:

To prevent crust from becoming soggy with cream pie, sprinkle crust with powdered sugar.

Baby Ruth Bars

The combination of peanut butter and chocolate makes these cookie bars irresistible.

3/4	**cup butter or margarine, softened**
1	**cup brown sugar**
1/4	**cup light corn syrup**
1	**teaspoon vanilla**
4	**cups oatmeal**
1/4	**cup smooth peanut butter**

Frosting:

6	**ounces chocolate chips**
3	**ounces butterscotch chips**
2/3	**cup peanut butter**

With electric mixer, blend together butter, brown sugar, corn syrup and vanilla.
Blend oats and peanut butter into mixture gradually.
Spread mixture into a very lightly greased 13 x 9-inch baking pan.
Bake in a 400 degree oven 15 minutes.

Frosting:
Melt chocolate and butterscotch chips, add peanut butter, blend quickly.
Spread on cookie mixture while still hot. Chill and cut into bars.

Yields approximately 2 dozen cookie bars

Harriet Kruman

Chewy Caramel Bars

These are easy, foolproof, delicious and a sure hit every time.

2 1/3	cups flour, divided
2	cups oatmeal
1	cup packed brown sugar
1	teaspoon baking soda
1/4	teaspoon salt
1	cup butter, melted
12	ounces semisweet chocolate chips
1 1/2	cups raisins (or chopped walnuts)
1	(12.25 ounce) jar of caramel hot fudge topping (or chocolate syrup)

Preheat oven to 350 degrees.
Combine 2 cups flour, oats, salt and baking soda in bowl of mixer, mix well.
With mixer on, slowly add butter to mixed dry ingredients, mix well. Reserve 1 cup.

Press remaining flour and oat mixture evenly into a 13 x 9-inch baking pan.
Bake until light golden, about 15 minutes.
Remove pan from oven, spread chocolate chips over baked crust.
Spread raisins over chips. Mix together remaining flour and caramel (or syrup).
Pour over raisins and chips, spreading over entire surface.

Spread reserved 1 cup crumb mixture over syrup.
Bake 20 to 25 minutes or until top is golden.
Remove from oven, cool, cut into squares and serve.

Yields 24 bars

Compliments of Richard Amster
Feature Food Editor, The Jewish Chronicle

Fruit and Chocolate Dreams

Sweet dreams are made of this rich confection.

1 1/4	cups flour
1/2	cup sugar
1/2	cup butter, softened

Topping:

2/3	cup flour
6	tablespoons sugar
6	tablespoons butter, softened
1/2	cup pecans, chopped
1/2	teaspoon vanilla extract
1/2	cup jam or jelly
1 1/2	cups chocolate chips

Preheat oven to 350 degrees.
Combine flour and sugar with pastry blender.
Cut in butter until mixture resembles fine crumbs.
Press into 9-inch square pan, bake 20 to 25 minutes.

Topping:
Mix flour, sugar, butter, pecans and vanilla with fork until mixture resembles coarse crumbs.
Remove pan from oven, spread with jam or jelly. Top with chocolate chips and crumb topping.

Bake 15 to 20 minutes longer.
Cool completely before cutting into squares.

Yields 16 squares

Sandy Oker

Chocolate Yum-Yum Bars

This is a yummy three layer cookie for lovers of chocolate.

First Layer:
1	egg, slightly beaten
1/2	cup butter, melted
1/3	cup cocoa
1/3	cup sugar
1	teaspoon vanilla
2	cups graham cracker crumbs
1/2	cup walnuts or pecans, chopped
1	cup flaked coconut

Second Layer:
1/4	cup butter, melted
3	tablespoons milk
2	tablespoons instant vanilla pudding powder
2	cups sifted powdered sugar

Third Layer:
4	ounces unsweetened chocolate, melted
1	tablespoon butter

First Layer:
Mix egg, butter, cocoa, sugar and vanilla over low heat until custard consistency.
Remove from heat, add graham crackers, nuts and coconut.
Pack into an ungreased 9 x 9-inch pan, refrigerate.

Second Layer:
Add milk to melted butter, stir in instant pudding and beat.
Add powdered sugar, beat until well blended.
Spread over first layer after it is firm and cool, refrigerate.

Third Layer:
Melt chocolate, add butter, drizzle over second layer and spread.
Allow to harden at room temperature. Cut into squares.

Yields 16 squares

Myra Judd

No-Bake Peanut Butter Squares

You won't believe something so simple to make tastes so good. These are a delicious addition to a snack or goodie tray anytime.

1	**cup brown sugar**
1	**cup dark corn syrup**
1	**cup peanut butter**
6	**cups toasted rice flake cereal**
12	**ounces chocolate chips, melted**

Dissolve brown sugar and corn syrup in sauce pan. Boil, stirring constantly.
Mix in peanut butter until dissolved.
Put cereal into a large bowl (I use Special K cereal).
Pour peanut butter mixture over, stir well to coat.

Place in a greased 10 x 15-inch jelly-roll pan, spreading out thin to cover pan.
Spread melted chocolate over top.
Refrigerate. Let stand before cutting into squares. Freezes well.

Yields 50 to 60 squares

Dee Selekman

Hint:
Tin coffee cans make excellent freezer container for cookies.

Ruth's Raspberry Ripples

This is a wonderful cookie bar offering any time of the year.

Cookie:
2	**cups flour**
1	**cup margarine or butter**
1/2	**cup sugar**
1/8	**teaspoon salt**
1	**egg yolk, beaten**

Filling:
1/2	**cup raspberry jam**
1/4	**cup sliced blanched almonds**
1/2	**teaspoon vanilla**

Combine flour, margarine, sugar and salt, blend to a coarse meal.
Add egg yolk, knead into a ball, divide into thirds.

Shape each third into a 12 x 1-inch strip.
Place about 4-inches apart on greased cookie sheet.
With spoon, form a canal down the center of the strips.
Mix filling ingredients together, spread evenly in canal.

Refrigerate 30 minutes.
Bake in 350 degree oven 20 to 25 minutes. Slice and cool.

Yields 36 bars

Lorraine Newman Mackler

Chocolate Chip Mandel Bread

Chocolate chips and nuts add richness to this classic.

3	eggs
3/4	cup sugar
3/4	cup oil
1	teaspoon almond extract
1	teaspoon vanilla extract
1/2	teaspoon lemon juice
2 1/2	cups flour
2	teaspoons baking powder
1	cup chopped nuts
1	cup chocolate chips

Beat eggs, sugar and oil, add extracts and lemon juice.
Add flour and baking powder, mix in chips and nuts.

Form dough into 3 rolls, approximately 2 x 12-inches.
Place on greased baking sheet, bake in 350 degree oven 25 to 30 minutes.
Remove and slice into 3/4-inch slices. Place on baking sheet, cut side up,
bake 10 minutes longer.

Yields approximately 2 1/2 dozen

Ruth Zaremberg

Kunitz Broit

A great back-to-basic mandel bread recipe. A perfect treat any time.

1 1/2	cups sugar
1/4	cup margarine
4	eggs
2	teaspoons vanilla
2	cups flour
1/2	teaspoon salt
1/2	teaspoon baking powder
3	cups chopped pecans

Cream together sugar and margarine, beat in eggs and vanilla.
Add flour, salt and baking powder, stir in pecans.

Pour mixture into 2 (9 x 5-inch) loaf pans coated with nonstick spray.
Bake in a 350 degree oven 30 to 40 minutes or until toothpick comes out clean.
Remove from pan and refrigerate overnight.

Slice into 1/4-inch slices, lay flat in single layer on ungreased cookie sheet.
Bake in a 375 degree oven 10 minutes or until golden brown.
Turn over, bake an additional 1 to 2 minutes.

Yields approximately 3 dozen

Sissie Margolis

Raisin Walnut Biscotti

This version of the Italian Biscotti is crisp and delicious. Try it dipped in coffee or tea.

1/4	**cup butter or margarine, softened**
2/3	**cup sugar**
2	**eggs**
1	**teaspoon vanilla**
2	**cups flour**
2	**teaspoons baking powder**
1	**teaspoon cinnamon**
1	**cup chopped walnuts**
1	**cup raisins**

Preheat oven to 350 degrees. Beat together butter, sugar, eggs and vanilla.
Stir in flour, baking powder and cinnamon, mix well.
Stir in walnuts and raisins.

Divide dough in half, shape into 2 long loaves, 1 1/2-inches in diameter.
Place on greased cookie sheets. Bake 18 to 20 minutes until firm.

Cut loaves into 3/4-inch diagonal slices.
Place cut side down on baking sheets.
Bake 10 minutes longer or until lightly browned.

Yields approximately 2 1/2 to 3 dozen cookies

Charilee Levy

Banana Chocolate Chip Cookies

Whip these up when you have a few ripe bananas around.

1 1/2	cups flour
1/2	teaspoon baking soda
3/4	teaspoon cinnamon
1	cup sugar
1/4	teaspoon nutmeg
3/4	cup shortening
1	egg, well beaten
1	cup mashed ripe bananas
1 3/4	cups oatmeal (not instant)
6	ounces semisweet chocolate chips

Sift together flour, baking soda, cinnamon, sugar and nutmeg. Cut in shortening.
Combine egg and banana, stir into mixture.
Add oatmeal and chips, mix until completely blended.

Drop by tablespoons onto ungreased cookie sheet. Bake in 400 degree oven 12 to 13 minutes.

Yields approximately 3 dozen

Shari Sweet

Chocolate Meringue Cookies

So delightful they disappear quickly.

3	egg whites, room temperature
1	cup sugar
1	teaspoon vanilla
1/2	teaspoon vinegar
3 1/2	tablespoons cocoa
1	(6 ounce) package semisweet chocolate chips

Beat egg whites until very stiff, add sugar while beating constantly.
Add vanilla and vinegar, continue beating. Stir in cocoa, add chocolate chips.

Drop by teaspoonfuls onto ungreased cookie sheet lined with waxed paper.
Bake in 275 degree oven 30 minutes.

Yields approximately 3 1/2 dozen

Eunice Baradon

Chocolate Delight

These are delicious, chewy, and easy to prepare.

1	cup raisins
1/2	cup walnuts
2	ounces unsweetened chocolate
1/2	cup butter
1 2/3	cups sugar
1	tablespoon vanilla
2	cups flour
2	teaspoons baking powder
1	teaspoon salt
1/3	cup milk
	Powdered sugar

Chop raisins and nuts in processor. Melt chocolate.
Blend butter, sugar and vanilla until soft and fluffy.
Stir raisins, nuts and melted chocolate into sugar mixture, mix well.

Sift flour with baking powder and salt.
Add to raisin mixture alternately with milk (start and end with flour).
Cover and chill several hours.

Shape into 1-inch balls, roll in powdered sugar.
Arrange 2-inches apart on lightly greased cookie sheet.
Bake in 350 degree oven 12 to 15 minutes, cool on a rack.

Yields approximately 3 dozen

Madeline Zukerman

Chocolate Snickerdoodles

These rated at the top of my daughter Margo's list of favorites.

1 1/2	cups sugar
1/2	cup margarine, softened
1	teaspoon vanilla
2	eggs
2 1/4	cups flour
1/2	cup cocoa
1/2	teaspoon baking powder
1/2	teaspoon baking soda
1/4	teaspoon salt
1/4	cup sugar
1	teaspoon cinnamon

Preheat oven to 400 degrees. Cream sugar and margarine until light and fluffy.
Blend in vanilla and eggs.
Add flour, cocoa, baking powder, baking soda and salt.

Roll dough into 1-inch balls.
Combine sugar and cinnamon, roll balls in mixture.
Bake 6 to 9 minutes on ungreased nonstick pan.

Yields approximately 4 dozen

Judy Kornblith

Fudgy Wudgy Chocolate Chip Deluxe Cookies

Absolutely awesome - for the most ardent chocolate fan.

2	cups butter
2	cups sugar
2	cups brown sugar
4	eggs
2	teaspoons vanilla
2	cups flour
2 1/2	cups oatmeal (process fine in blender)
2	teaspoons baking powder
2	teaspoons baking soda
1	teaspoon salt
1	(8 ounce) chocolate bar, grated
24	ounces semisweet chocolate morsels
3	cups nuts, chopped

Preheat oven to 350 degrees.
Cream butter and both sugars, add eggs and vanilla.
Combine flour, oatmeal, baking powder, soda and salt.
Gradually add to butter sugar mix.
Add grated chocolate, morsels and nuts. Refrigerate 30 minutes.

Drop by teaspoonfuls onto prepared cookie sheet, press flat. Bake 15 minutes.

Yields approximately 6 1/2 dozen

Judy Papernick

Hamentaschen

The kind your grandmother made during Purim. Enjoy them with a glass of milk.

2	eggs
1/2	cup oil
1/2	teaspoon vanilla
1/3	cup orange juice
3 1/2	cups flour
3	teaspoons baking powder
1/2	teaspoon salt
3/4	cup sugar
	Cherry, apricot, prune, or poppyseed pie filling, chocolate chips, nuts

Beat eggs (may substitute egg beaters) add oil, vanilla and juice, mix well.
Combine flour, baking powder, salt and sugar, add to egg mixture.
Wrap dough in waxed paper, refrigerate 2 hours or overnight.

Preheat oven to 375 degrees.
Roll out to 1/8 - 1/4-inch thickness, cut into 3-inch circles.
Place 1 teaspoon of filling in center of circle.
Fold into triangles, by pinching sides up to meet in center over filling.
Bake on a greased cookie sheet 10 to 15 minutes.

Yields approximately 3 dozen

Charlotte Helfer

Marble Drop Cookies

Cookies are a favorite with everyone, a great alternative to cakes as a dessert.

2	cups flour
1/2	teaspoon baking powder
1/4	teaspoon salt
1/2	cup light brown sugar, packed
1/2	cup sugar
1/2	cup salted butter, softened
1	large egg
1/2	cup sour cream
1	teaspoon vanilla
6	ounces semisweet chocolate chips

In medium bowl, combine flour, baking powder and salt, set aside.
Combine sugars in large bowl using an electric mixer at medium speed.
Add butter, beat until batter is grainy.
Add egg, sour cream and vanilla.
Beat at medium speed until light and fluffy, scrape bowl.
Add flour mixture, blend at low speed until just combined. (Do not over mix.)

Melt chocolate chips in double boiler over hot (not boiling) water.
Stir constantly until melted.
Cool chocolate a few minutes, pour over cookie batter.
Lightly fold melted chocolate into dough, just enough to create marble streaks.

Drop by rounded tablespoons onto ungreased cookie sheets, 2-inches apart.
Bake in a preheated 300 degree oven 20 to 22 minutes.
Do not brown. Transfer to rack to cool.

Yields 2 1/2 dozen

Charilee Levy

Nana's Sugar Cookies

This is the recipe I use to bake Chanukah cookies with my grandchildren, just as I did with my grandmother, Nana. Enjoy!

1 1/2	**cups sugar**
1/2	**cup butter or margarine**
2	**eggs**
2	**cups flour**
2	**teaspoons baking powder**
1	**teaspoon vanilla**
	Nuts, chocolate jimmies, colored sugars for topping

Cream together sugar and butter. Add eggs and mix well.
Sift together flour and baking powder, add to mixture. Add vanilla.
Wrap dough in plastic wrap, chill several hours or overnight.

Preheat oven to 350 degrees.
Roll out to 1/8-inch on floured surface (preferably a chilled pastry board).
Lightly sprinkle additional flour on dough before cutting desired shapes.
(This is a very sticky dough.)

Place cookies on cookie sheets lined with parchment paper.
Sprinkle with nuts, jimmies and sugar before baking (or bake plain and ice when cool).
Bake until golden, about 7 minutes, depending on oven and shape of cookie.

Yields approximately 3 dozen cookies

Marlene Silverman

Aunt Gussie's Cookie Dough Strudel

My Aunt Gussie was famous for this wonderful strudel. The nuts add crunch, the preserves and raisins, color and texture. Not only do they make a delicious combination, but they call to mind wonderful memories of sweet treats shared with loved ones.

1 1/4	cups sugar
1/2	cup oil
2	eggs
1	teaspoon vanilla
1/3	cup orange juice
4-4 1/2	cups sifted flour
3	teaspoons baking powder
1/8	teaspoon salt
1	(6 ounce) jar grape jam
1	(6 ounce) jar apricot preserves
1 1/2	cups raisins
2	cups walnuts, chopped
1/4	cup milk
	Cinnamon and sugar

By hand, cream sugar, oil and eggs. Add vanilla and orange juice.
In separate bowl, combine flour, baking powder and salt.
Add slowly to sugar mixture, mixing well after each addition (dough should not be sticky).
Cover and refrigerate at least 2 hours or overnight.

Divide dough into 3 or 4 pieces.
Roll each section into an 8 x 14-inch rectangle, approximately 1/4-inch thick.
Spread with jellies, nuts, raisins, cinnamon and sugar. Roll up jelly roll style.

Place on cookie sheets sprayed with nonstick spray.
Mark for slicing with a sharp knife about l-inch apart and 1/4-inch deep.
Brush with milk, sprinkle sugar and cinnamon on top.
Bake in 350 degree oven 15 to 20 minutes until brown.

Cool 3 minutes, slide spatula underneath to loosen, cool 5 minutes longer.
Cut into slices, cool completely.

Note: Amount of filling is your choice - if filled too full it will leak out of the sides.

Yields 2 dozen

Sheila Glasser

213

Deep-Dish Pear Cobbler

Summer or winter, this fruit dessert topped with a biscuit crust is a winner.

Filling:

4 1/2	cups peeled and sliced pears (peaches or apples)
1	cup sugar
3	tablespoons flour
3/4	teaspoon cinnamon
1/2	cup pecans (optional)

Topping:

1 1/2	cups flour
3	tablespoons sugar
2 1/4	teaspoons baking powder
3/4	teaspoon salt
1/2	cup oil
4	tablespoons milk
1	egg

Preheat oven to 350 degrees.

Combine pears, sugar, flour, cinnamon and pecans.

Arrange evenly in an ungreased 9 x 9-inch pan.

Combine dry topping ingredients. Add oil, milk, egg until just blended.

Spoon topping over fruit to create 9 sections.

Bake uncovered 25 minutes until top is brown and filling is bubbly.

Serves 9

Judy Kornblith

Blueberry Tart

A food processor makes this an easy to prepare tart for blueberry lovers.

1 1/4	cups flour
1/2	cup butter or margarine
2	tablespoons sour cream
1 1/2	cups frozen unsweetened blueberries (thawed and rinsed)

Topping:

3	large egg yolks
1/3	cup sour cream
3/4	cup sugar
1/4	cup flour

Preheat oven to 375 degrees.
In food processor, blend flour and butter.
Add sour cream and process until ball forms. Remove, flatten into a disk.
Place in center of ungreased 9-inch springform pan.
Press over bottom and up sides.
Bake until set (but not brown), 20 minutes.
Reduce heat to 350 degrees.

Arrange blueberries in shell (does not have to be cool).
Without washing food processor, process all topping ingredients until just blended.
Pour topping over berries.

Bake 40 to 45 minutes until top is golden and meringue-like.
Cool on wire rack, remove sides of pan.
Serve warm or at room temperature.

Serves 8

Beverly Robins

Pecan Raisin Tart

This extra scrumptious crust made with a mixture of ground pecans and flour, combined with the nut-raisin filling, gives this tart an enticing nutty flavor.

Crust:

1 1/3	cups flour
1/4	cup pecans
1/4	cup sugar
1/2	cup unsalted margarine, chilled
1	egg yolk
3	tablespoons water (approximate)

Filling:

1/2	cup unsalted margarine
1/2	cup light corn syrup
1/2	cup packed dark brown sugar
3	large eggs
1 1/2	teaspoons vanilla extract
2	cups pecans, coarsely chopped
1/2	cup raisins

Crust:

Blend flour, pecans and sugar in processor until finely ground.
Add butter, pulse processor until mixture resembles coarse meal.
Add egg yolk, process until blended.
Blend in enough water by tablespoons until dough begins to form clumps.
Remove, gather into a ball, flatten into a disk, wrap in plastic wrap.
Chill 2 hours.

Preheat oven to 350 degrees.
Roll out dough on lightly floured surface to a 12-inch circle.
Transfer to tart pan with removable bottom.
Press into pan, trim off excess dough, seal cracks with dough scraps.
Line crust with foil. Lay pie weights or dry beans on foil, bake 15 minutes.

Remove foil and weights, bake until crust is pale golden, about 14 minutes.
Pierce with fork if bubbles form. Transfer to a rack and cool.

Pecan Raisin Tart, continued

Filling:
Combine margarine, corn syrup and brown sugar in heavy saucepan.
Stir over medium heat until melted and smooth. Cool slightly.

Whisk eggs and vanilla in large bowl to blend. Stir in pecans and raisins.
Stir in margarine and sugar mixture. Pour filling into crust.
Bake until filling is almost set, about 35 minutes. Cool on rack.

Serves 8

Harriet Kruman

Old-Fashioned Rice Pudding

Another trend in the dessert world has been the resurgence of homey comforting treats - this looks and tastes like a lot more work.

2/3	**cup quick-cooking rice**
2 3/4	**cups milk**
1/3	**cup sugar**
1	**tablespoon butter or margarine**
1/2	**teaspoon salt**
1/2	**teaspoon vanilla**
1/4	**teaspoon nutmeg (optional)**
1	**teaspoon cinnamon**
	Cinnamon and sugar to taste

Combine all ingredients in greased 1 quart baking dish.
Bake in 350 degree oven 15 minutes, stir.
Bake 45 minutes longer. Place under broiler to brown.

Sprinkle with cinnamon and sugar to taste. Serve warm or chilled.

Note: As it cools, the pudding will thicken as the rice continues to absorb liquid.

Serves 3 to 4

Rosalyn Wein

Chef Dave's Easy Pecan Bread Pudding

Rich and soothing - your guests will declare it was well worth your excursion into this part of the dessert world.

5	**eggs**
2	**cups sugar**
3	**teaspoons vanilla extract**
2	**teaspoons nutmeg**
2	**teaspoons cinnamon**
1/2	**cup melted butter**
3	**cups milk**
1	**cup golden raisins (or your favorite dried fruit, no citrus)**
3/4	**cups chopped pecans**
8	**cups stale Italian bread cubes**

In mixing bowl, beat eggs until foamy.
Add sugar, vanilla, nutmeg, cinnamon and butter, mix well.
Beat in milk, stir in raisins and pecans.

In a greased 13 x 9-inch baking pan place bread cubes.
Pour milk mixture over bread, stir until well saturated.
Set aside until liquid appears around edges of pan.

Bake in 350 degree oven 35 to 40 minutes.
Raise heat to 425 degrees.
Bake 15 to 20 minutes longer or until golden brown.
Cool, cut into squares. Serve with whipped topping.

Serves 8 to 10

Compliments of Chef David Conley
Poli Restaurant

Moré Tiramisu

Cake soaked in brandy and coffee, dusted with cocoa, rich with cheese - a perfect finale.

4	eggs, separated
4	tablespoons sugar
8	ounces cream cheese, softened
1	cup espresso coffee (see Note)
2	tablespoons sugar
1/2	cup coffee flavored liqueur (optional)
1/2	cup cocoa powder or chocolate shavings
1	pound sponge or pound cake, cut up

Beat egg yolks and sugar at medium speed until lemon colored.
Add soft cream cheese and cream well.

In another bowl, using clean and very cold beaters, beat egg whites and a sprinkle of sugar until thick, but not stiff.
Fold egg whites into the cheese mixture.
Combine espresso, sugar and liqueur.

Layer the bottom of a 9 x 9-inch pan with cake.
Using pastry bush, wet each piece of cake well with the coffee mixture.
Pour half of cheese mixture over wet cake.
Sprinkle with half of cocoa or chocolate shavings. Repeat.
Chill until firm.

Note: If using instant granules, use 1 tablespoon coffee and 1 cup boiling water

Serves 8

Compliments of Chef Louie Moré
Moré Restaurant

Rice Pudding with Fruit

A delicately flavored dairy dessert.

1/3	cup converted white rice
1/2	cup cold water
1/2	cup milk
1/4	cup golden raisins
1	small apple, peeled and sliced
1	teaspoon vanilla
2	teaspoons sugar
	Salt to taste
1	tablespoon butter or margarine

Mix all ingredients in a greased 1 quart baking dish.
Cover and bake in 350 degree oven 50 minutes to 1 hour.
Stir rice every 15 minutes. (Add a little milk if too dry.)

Serves 2 to 3

Gertrude Mallinger

Bernie's Coffee Ice Cream Cake

This can be made in advance and frozen for weeks.

1	cup very strong coffee (may be instant)
36	large marshmallows
2	(12 ounce) containers frozen whipped topping, thawed
2	packages unfilled lady fingers
	Chocolate shavings (garnish)

In a small saucepan combine coffee and marshmallows.
Melt over medium heat, stirring constantly.
Cool slightly, fold in 1 carton of whipped topping, set aside.

Line the bottom and sides of a 9-inch springform pan with lady fingers.
Pour coffee mixture into prepared pan, refrigerate until set.
Top with remaining whipped topping, sprinkle with chocolate shavings.

Serves 8 to 10

Bernice Friedlander

Chocolate Pizza

A fun treat for both kids and adults.

1	(12 ounce) package semisweet chocolate chips
1	pound white almond bark, divided
2	cups miniature marshmallows
1	cup crispy rice cereal
1	cup peanuts
1	(6 ounce) jar red maraschino cherries, drained, halved
3	tablespoons green maraschino cherries, drained, quartered
1/3	cup sweetened, flaked coconut
1	teaspoon oil

Combine chips and 14 ounces of the almond bark in a 2 quart microwave bowl.
Microwave on high 2 minutes, stir.
Continue cooking for 1 to 2 minutes or until smooth, stirring every 30 seconds.
Mix in marshmallows, cereal and peanuts.
Pour mixture onto greased 12-inch pizza pan.
Top with cherries, sprinkle with coconut.

Combine remaining 2 ounces almond bark with oil in small glass measuring cup.
Microwave for 1 minute, stir.
Continue cooking for 30 to 60 seconds or until smooth, stirring every 15 seconds.
Drizzle over coconut, refrigerate until firm. Serve at room temperature.

Serves 8 to 10

Sandy Oker

Lemon Sorbet

Sorbets are all the rage lately, offering a rich frozen treat without the fat of ice cream. This sorbet is especially attractive served in hollowed-out lemon, lime or orange halves; or small scoops may be placed on scored lemon or orange slices.

1	**cup sugar**
1	**cup water**
2-2 1/4	**cups fresh lemon juice**
	Zest of 3 lemons, minced
2	**egg whites**

Combine sugar and water in small saucepan over medium-high heat.
Stir until sugar is dissolved.
Remove from heat just before mixture boils.
Cool slightly, cover and chill syrup.

Combine syrup, lemon juice and zest, blend well.
Place in ice cream maker and freeze partially so sorbet is still soft.
Add egg whites and complete churning.

If using conventional freezer, turn mixture into metal container and freeze.
Thaw partially, spoon into food processor, beat until smooth and fluffy.
Add egg whites, continue mixing until well blended, refreeze.

Yields 1 quart

Carol Lederer

Hint:
Lemons: store whole lemons in a tightly sealed jar of water in the refrigerator. They will yield much more juice than when first purchased.

PASSOVER

PASSOVER

Baked Salmon Loaf with Carrot Topping

A delicious classic served anytime by popular demand. This is one of those 'mom' dishes that bring back wonderful memories.

1	**(14 3/4 ounce) can red salmon**
1/2	**cup sour cream**
1	**onion, grated**
	Juice of 1/2 lemon
2	**eggs, beaten**
2	**teaspoons matzo meal**
1/8	**teaspoon pepper**
1	**carrot, grated**
	Margarine
	Paprika

Mix everything together except carrot, margarine and paprika.
Shape into loaf and put into baking dish.
Sprinkle grated carrot on loaf, top with margarine and paprika.
Bake in a 350 degree oven for 30 to 45 minutes.

Serves 4

Lea Davidson

Cupcake Blintzes

An easy adoption of a traditional dish making them ideal for entertaining. Everyone loves them!

1	**pound creamed cottage cheese**
1/4	**cup butter, melted**
3/4	**cup sugar**
1/2	**cup matzo cake meal (scant)**
4	**eggs, beaten (can use egg substitute)**

Mix together cottage cheese, butter, sugar and cake meal. Add eggs.
Grease muffin tins, fill 3/4 full.
Bake in a 350 degree oven 40 to 45 minutes for large muffin tins.
(Reduce baking time if using smaller tins.)
Serve with sour cream or jelly.

Yields 24

Ilene Fingeret

Chicken Breast Stuffed with Farfel and Vegetables

This is one of my favorite Passover dinner dishes. It is easy to assemble-roast and serve straight from the oven.

1	**cup margarine**
3	**cloves garlic, crushed**
20	**chicken breast halves, boneless, skin on**
1	**large onion, chopped**
4	**stalks celery, chopped**
2	**carrots, grated**
1/2	**pound mushrooms, sliced**
1/2	**cup oil**
8	**cups matzo farfel**
2	**eggs**
1/2	**cup chopped parsley**
	Chicken broth (for moistening)
1/4	**cup wine**
1	**(10 1/2 ounce) can kosher mushroom soup**

Melt margarine and add crushed garlic.
Dip chicken breasts in margarine and garlic.

Sauté vegetables in oil.
Mix farfel and eggs together. Add parsley and sautéed vegetables.
Add enough chicken broth to moisten, mix well.
Use your hands to form a ball of stuffing.
Mold each chicken breast around stuffing balls.
Place in a large foil pan, touching each other.

Cover, bake in a 350 degree oven, 1 hour and 15 minutes.
Combine wine and mushroom soup, pour over chicken.
Bake, uncovered, 25 minutes longer, until brown.

Serves 20

Marlene Gelman

Orange and Apricot Stuffed Capon with Brandy Glaze

The unusual combination of flavors make this a special elegant company dish. When you taste this, you will know it is well worth the effort.

Stuffing:

4	cups matzo farfel
1	cup orange juice
1/4	cup margarine
1/3	cup chopped onion
1/3	cup chopped celery
1/3	cup chopped red pepper
1	egg, lightly beaten
1/2	cup golden raisins (or diced apricots)
1/2	teaspoon salt
1/2	teaspoon grated orange zest
1	(8 pound) capon
	Salt, pepper, garlic powder and onion powder to taste

Glaze:

3/4	cup apricot jam
6	tablespoons orange juice
2	tablespoons brandy

In large bowl, soak farfel in orange juice.
In skillet, melt margarine, sauté onions, celery, and red pepper until soft.
Add sautéed vegetables to farfel.
Stir in egg, raisins, salt and orange zest, mix well.

Sprinkle neck and body cavity of capon with seasonings.
Spoon stuffing loosely into neck and body cavities.
Place capon on rack in shallow roasting pan, breast side up.
Sprinkle with additional seasonings.

Combine glaze ingredients, mix well. Brush capon with glaze.
Roast in 350 degree oven 2 hours, basting with glaze every 30 minutes.
Combine pan drippings with remaining glaze, skim fat off surface.
Serve capon with sauce.

Serves 6

Lisa Steindel

Festive Vegetable Cutlets

This is an impressive mouth-watering combination of ingredients that can be used for Passover.

1 1/2-2	cups minced red or yellow peppers (or a mixture of both)
2	tablespoons olive oil
1 1/2	cups grated carrots (4 carrots)
1/2	pound raw spinach, cleaned, chopped (2 tightly packed cups)
3	medium potatoes, boiled and mashed (2 cups)
6	tablespoons grated onion (1 large)
3	eggs, lightly beaten
1 1/2	teaspoons salt
	Freshly ground black pepper to taste
1	cup matzo meal
	Vegetable oil

Sauté peppers in olive oil until soft.
Add all remaining ingredients except vegetable oil.
Let mixture stand 30 minutes or overnight, refrigerated.
(Bring to room temperature before continuing.)
You can fry or bake cutlets.

Fry:
Heat 1/4-inch of vegetable oil in a large skillet.
Form each patty with about 1/4 cup of the mixture.
Flatten patties slightly, fry in batches.
Cook 6 minutes on first side, turn, fry 3 or 4 minutes longer.
Drain on paper towels and serve immediately.

Bake:
Place patties on lightly greased baking sheet.
Bake in a preheated 350 degree oven for about 10 minutes.
Turn patties, bake 7 to 10 minutes longer.

Yields 40 patties

Serves 6 to 8

Charilee Levy

Lasagna with Mozzarella and Cottage Cheese

A departure from the ordinary, this lasagna is a rich, easy, main or luncheon dish for family or company during Passover.

7-8	whole matzos
2	pounds cottage cheese
4	eggs
1/4	teaspoon garlic powder
1	(15 ounce) jar spaghetti sauce
1	pound mozzarella cheese

Spray a 9 x 13-inch pan with nonstick spray.
Pour boiling water over matzo in colander to slightly soften, drain.
Mix together cottage cheese, eggs and garlic powder.
Begin layering with sauce, matzo, cheese mixture and mozzarella cheese.
This will make 4 layers.
Bake in a 325 degree oven 45 minutes.

Serves 6

Nancy Neudorf

Pear and Prune Tzimmes

Loosely translated from Yiddish, tzimmes means "a fuss over something," but in culinary terms, it's commonly a casserole of various fruits, vegetables and/or meats.

10	ripe Anjou pears, peeled, sliced
1	pound pitted prunes, halved
4	tablespoons lemon juice
1	tablespoon honey
	Cinnamon to taste

Spread pear slices in a greased 9 x 13-inch baking pan.
Arrange prunes on top.
Drizzle with lemon juice, honey and sprinkle with cinnamon.
Bake, covered, in a preheated 350 degree oven 30 minutes.
Uncover, bake 20 minutes longer.
Serve hot or warm as a side dish.

Serves 12

Marianne Silberman

Macaroni and Creamy Cheddar Cheese Bake

An impressive luncheon or light supper entrée, a treat during Passover. This recipe has a contemporary twist, and satisfies just like the macaroni of childhood.

4	**eggs, divided**
4 1/2-5	**cups farfel**
1	**cup milk**
1	**teaspoon salt**
1/2	**pound Cheddar cheese, cubed**
1/4	**cup butter, cubed**

Grease a 2 quart casserole.
Whisk 3 eggs, pour over farfel and mix.
In another bowl, beat one egg, stir in milk and salt.

Layer casserole with 1/2 of farfel mixture, 1/2 the cheese, distribute butter evenly.
Add remaining farfel, cheese, and pour milk mixture evenly over top.
Cover and bake in a 350 degree oven 30 minutes.
Remove cover, bake 10 to 15 minutes longer until brown. Cut into squares.

Serves 4 to 6

Sheri Minkoff

Charoset Sephardic Style

Finely chopped dates and apple, moistened with wine to represent the morsel of sweetness to lighten the burden of unhappy memory.

10	**ounces pitted dates**
1	**Red Delicious apple, peeled, cored and quartered**
1/4	**cup sweet red wine**
2	**teaspoons cinnamon**

Process all ingredients in food processor until smooth.

Yields 2 cups

Rachel Kalnicki

Derma

'Over the river and through the woods to Grandmother's house we go....'

1/2	cup grated carrots
1	large chopped onion
1/2	cup finely chopped celery
2	cloves garlic, crushed
1/4	teaspoon poultry seasoning
3	cups crushed egg matzo
1	cup margarine, melted
1	teaspoon salt
1/4	teaspoon pepper

Combine all ingredients in large bowl, mix well.
Place a 20-inch piece of aluminum foil on a cookie sheet.
Shape mixture into a 16-inch roll. Place on foil.

Bring 2 long sides up over derma, fold down loosely in a series of locked folds.
(This permits heat circulation and expansion.)
Fold short ends up and over again, crimp to seal.
Bake in a preheated 350 degree oven 45 minutes.
Unwrap and cut while hot into 1/2-inch thick slices.

Serves 6

Rachel Kalnicki

Harvest Vegetable Tzimmes

This is a child-friendly vegetarian entrée. You may substitute raisins for the prunes or just omit the dried fruit.

1/2	**pound carrots, 1/2-inch slices**
1/2	**pound parsnips, 1/2-inch slices**
1	**pound sweet potatoes or yams, peeled, thinly sliced**
1	**onion, cut in 1/2, sliced 1/4-inch slivers**
1	**cup orange juice**
	Water
3	**tablespoons potato starch**
1/2	**cup honey**
1/2	**cup pitted prunes, coarsely chopped**
2	**teaspoons grated ginger**
	Kosher salt and white pepper to taste

In 3 quart saucepan, combine carrots, parsnips, potatoes and onion.
Add orange juice and barely enough water to cover vegetables.
Bring to boil over high heat. Reduce, simmer 20 to 25 minutes or until almost tender.
Drain, reserve 3/4 cup cooking liquid.
Slowly add potato starch to reserved liquid, blending well.

Place cooked vegetables in a 13 x 9-inch baking dish.
Pour potato starch mixture and honey over vegetables.
Add prunes, ginger, salt and pepper, stir well.
Bake, uncovered, in a 375 degree oven, 50 minutes until brown, stirring occasionally.
(Sauce should be thick and vegetables tender.)

Serves 6

Joan Wagman

Maxine's Passover Carrot Pudding

This rich tasting, elegant-yet homey pudding is delightful to look at, delicious to eat and easy to assemble, Passover or anytime.

3	**cups grated carrots**
3/4	**cup matzo meal**
2	**eggs, beaten**
1/4	**cup minced onion**
1	**teaspoon salt**
2	**tablespoons margarine, melted**
1	**(14 1/2 ounce) can chicken broth, undiluted**
2	**teaspoons minced parsley**

Combine all ingredients and stir.
Pour into a 1 1/2 quart greased casserole.
Bake, uncovered, in a 325 degree oven 50 minutes.

Serves 6

Sheila Glasser

Nathan's Sephardic Charoset

This is a traditional recipe of the Sephardic Jews from Turkey and is a vital part of the Seder.

1	**pound raw unsalted cashews**
1/2	**pound pitted dates**
2	**teaspoons orange zest**
1/2	**cup light sweet red wine**
2	**bananas**
	Cinnamon to taste

Chop cashews, dates and orange zest in food processor.
Add wine slowly to blend.
Blend in remaining ingredients to form a soft paste.

Note: Add more or less wine for desired consistency.

Yields 1 quart

Harriet Kruman

Passover "Hot Rolls"

Everyone looks forward to the special Passover delicacies and switching from bread to crisp "matzoh." After a few days of eating "matzoh" we crave something that will remind us of bread. These "rolls" may be split and used for sandwiches.

2	cups matzo meal
1	teaspoon salt
1	tablespoon sugar
1	cup water
1/2	cup peanut oil
4	eggs

Combine matzo meal with salt and sugar.
Bring water and oil to boil.
Add to matzo meal mixture and mix well.
Beat in eggs thoroughly, one at a time.
Allow to stand 15 minutes.

With oiled hands, shape into rolls.
Place on a well-greased cookie sheet.
Bake in a 375 degree oven 40 to 50 minutes or until golden brown.

Yields 12 Rolls

Ruth Foreman

Spinach Vegetable Kugel

A potpourri of exquisite garden ingredients.

2	cups chopped onion
1	cup chopped celery
1	cup chopped mushrooms
3/4	cup margarine
3	cups grated carrots
1 1/2	cups matzo meal
2	(1 pound) packages frozen chopped spinach, thawed, drained
6	eggs, beaten
	Salt and pepper to taste

Sauté onion, celery and mushrooms in margarine 10 minutes, stirring often.
Add all remaining ingredients.
Pour into a 9 x 13-inch greased pan.
Bake in 350 degree oven, uncovered, 40 to 45 minutes until firm.
(Do not over bake, or will become too dry.) Cool before cutting.

Serves 8

Elinor Zaremberg

Hint:

To change a recipe to pareve that is designated meat because it uses a meat-based
broth, substitute vegetable broth.

Sweet Apple Matzo Kugel

Dense with apples, nuts and raisins, this kugel is as nutritious as it is delicious.

4	**matzos**
3	**eggs**
1/2	**teaspoon salt**
1/2	**cup sugar**
1/4	**cup margarine**
1	**teaspoon cinnamon**
1/2	**cup nuts, chopped**
2-3	**apples, peeled and chopped**
1/2	**cup raisins**
	Additional margarine as needed

Break matzos and soak in water until soft, drain (do not squeeze dry).
Beat eggs with salt, sugar, margarine and cinnamon. Add matzo.
Stir in chopped nuts, apples and raisins.

Pour mixture into a greased 9 x 13-inch casserole.
Dot top with additional margarine.
Bake in a 350 degree oven 45 minutes.

Serves 8

Ilene Fingeret

Hint:

Low-fat: When cooking low-fat recipes, you'll get the best results if you use a saucepan or skillet with a nonstick surface.

Vegetable Kugel with Broccoli and Mushrooms

Don't be afraid to dress up a traditional dish with a little excitement. Vegetables make this kugel side dish different and delicious.

3	cups matzo farfel
3	cups chicken broth (heated)
2	tablespoons oil
2	onions, sliced
2	stalks celery, sliced
1	cup sliced mushrooms
2	cups broccoli, small florets
2	cups cooked chicken, sliced (optional)
3	eggs
	Salt, pepper, garlic powder, paprika to taste

Combine farfel and broth in bowl, set aside.
Heat oil in large skillet.
Add vegetables and brown quickly over high heat.
Add chicken if desired.

Beat eggs, add all ingredients to farfel and broth.
Mix well and season to taste.
Put in well-greased 2 quart casserole.
Bake uncovered, in 350 degree oven 1 hour or until browned.

Note: May prepare in muffin tins and bake for 45 minutes.

Serves 8 to 10

Judy Papernick

Apple Cake with Cinnamon and Walnuts

An "Old World" recipe for you and your family to enjoy and cherish.

6	eggs
1 1/2	cups sugar
2/3	cup oil
1 1/2	cups matzo cake meal
5	apples, sliced

Topping:

1	cup chopped walnuts
1	teaspoon cinnamon
2/3	cup sugar

Beat eggs, sugar and oil. Add cake meal and beat well.
Grease 9 x 13-inch pan. Combine topping ingredients.
Pour in 1/2 the batter, 1/2 the apples and 1/2 the topping. Repeat.
Bake in 350 degree oven for 1 hour and 15 minutes.

Serves 8

Ruth Fauman-Fichman

Hint:

Strawberries: cut strawberries horizontally if using berries whose flavor is disappointing. More surface is exposed and more juice comes out.

Banana Walnut Cake with Chocolate Chips

There are banana cakes and nut cakes, but this superb combination is one in a million.

8	eggs, separated
1/4	teaspoon salt
1 1/2	cups sugar, divided
2	large ripe bananas, mashed
1	tablespoon lemon juice
1/2	cup potato starch
1/2	cup matzo cake meal
1/2	cup finely chopped walnuts
1/2	cup semisweet chocolate chips

Preheat oven to 350 degrees.
In large bowl of an electric mixer, beat egg yolks with salt 1 minute.
Gradually add 3/4 cup sugar, beat 3 minutes.
Add bananas and lemon juice slowly, beat 3 minutes longer.

Sift potato starch and cake meal together.
Fold in very carefully with a rubber spatula.
Beat egg whites until foamy, gradually add remaining sugar.
Beat until whites are stiff, but not dry.
Fold whites gently into yolk mixture, fold in nuts and chocolate chips.

Bake in an ungreased, 10-inch tube pan for 1 hour.
Reduce heat to 300 degrees and bake 10 minutes longer.
Invert immediately and cool completely. May be frozen.

Serves 12

Shari Sweet

Chocolate Walnut Torte

This torte is always a sensation, whenever it is served! The semisweet chocolate, walnuts and apples make a heavenly combination.

6	**eggs, separated**
1 1/2	**cups sugar**
1	**cup chopped walnuts**
2	**Red Delicious apples, peeled, cored and grated**
1/2	**cup matzo meal**
4	**ounces semisweet chocolate, grated**
	Powdered sugar (garnish)

Preheat oven to 350 degrees.

Beat egg yolks with sugar until light and creamy.

Gently stir in walnuts, apples, matzo meal and chocolate.

Beat egg whites until they form stiff peaks (but not dry).

Fold into egg yolk mixture gently, (but thoroughly) using a rubber spatula.

Pour mixture into a 9-inch springform pan.

Bake 45 minutes to 1 hour or until cake springs back when pressed lightly.

Cool in pan. Serve sprinkled with powdered sugar.

Serves 8 to 10

Rachel Kalnecki

Crispy Honey Cake Cookies

The measuring and the instructions are so easy that children love to make and eat these very rich, very different, very good cookies. This honey, nut and raisin version is a real winner.

1	**egg**
2	**tablespoons oil**
	Water
1	**(12 ounce) package honey cake mix**
1	**tablespoon instant coffee**
1	**cup chopped nuts**
1	**cup raisins**

Break egg into a 1 cup measuring cup, add oil.
Add enough water to measure 1/2 cup, beat well.

In another bowl, combine cake mix and coffee.
Add liquid ingredients, stir, add nuts and raisins, mix well.

Spray a cookie sheet with nonstick spray. Drop by teaspoonfuls, flatten.
Bake in a 325 degree oven 10 to 15 minutes.
Cool slightly, store in an airtight container.

Yields 2 dozen

Sheila Glasser

Flourless Chocolate Cake

A grand climax to a Passover meal, a cut above classic and outrageously delicious.

1 2/3	**cups semisweet chocolate chips**
7	**tablespoons unsalted butter**
7	**eggs, separated**
1/3	**cup sugar**

Preheat oven to 275 degrees.
Butter and flour a 10-inch springform pan (use potato starch for flour).
In top of a double boiler, melt chocolate and butter until smooth.
Remove from heat.

In mixing bowl, beat egg whites until slightly stiff.
Add sugar, beat 30 seconds until stiff.

Whisk egg yolks into slightly cooled chocolate mixture.
Gently fold chocolate mixture into egg whites (mix only until no white streaks remain).
Pour batter into pan, bake 30 to 40 minutes. Release sides of pan, cool on a wire rack.

Serves 12

Shari Sweet

Frozen Strawberry Meringue Torte

Refreshing and luscious with the flavors and texture of seasonal fruit.

Crust:

1 1/2	cups almond macaroons
2	teaspoons margarine, melted
1/2	cup chopped walnuts or pecans

Filling:

2	egg whites, room temperature
1	cup sugar
2	cups fresh sliced strawberries
1	tablespoon lemon juice

Sauce:

1	(10 ounce) package frozen sliced strawberries
3	tablespoons frozen orange juice concentrate, undiluted
1	tablespoon currant jelly

Preheat oven to 350 degrees.
Process macaroons, margarine and nuts until mixture holds together.
Press into a 10-inch springform pan. Bake 7 to 10 minutes. Cool.

Beat filling ingredients on low speed until well blended.
Increase speed to high, beat until stiff peaks form (about 10 to 15 minutes).
Pour into cooled crust. Cover and freeze until firm, about 6 hours.

(This may be frozen up to three weeks and served directly from freezer.)
When ready to serve, puree sauce ingredients together. Pour over each
frozen slice of the torte.

Serves 12

Marianne Silberman

Spicy Carrot Cake with Toasted Almonds

X-rated. Extra good, extra fine, and extra compliments for the chef!

1	**cup carrot puree (4 to 6 carrots)**
6	**eggs, separated**
1 1/2	**cups sugar**
1	**teaspoon vanilla**
2	**tablespoons orange juice (or orange liqueur)**
1/4	**cup matzo meal**
1/4	**cup matzo cake meal**
1 1/4	**cups ground toasted almonds or hazelnuts**
1	**teaspoon cinnamon**
1/4	**teaspoon ginger**
1/4	**teaspoon nutmeg**
1/4	**teaspoon allspice**
	Zest of 1 lemon, finely grated
	Pinch of salt

Carrot Puree:
Boil 4 to 6 medium carrots in water until tender.
Process in a food mill or mash well with fork. Set aside.

Lightly grease and line 10-inch springform pan with parchment paper.
Beat egg yolks, slowly add sugar until mixture thickens.
Blend in vanilla, juice, matzo meals, nuts, spices and lemon zest.

Whip egg whites with salt until foamy.
Increase speed, whip until firm peaks form.
Stir carrot puree into egg yolk mixture.
Fold 1/3 of the beaten egg whites into yolk mixture to lighten it.
In two more additions, fold remaining whites gently into batter.

Spoon into prepared pan, place in a preheated 350 degree oven.
Immediately reduce heat to 325 degrees.
Bake 50 to 60 minutes, until cake springs back when lightly pressed.

Serves 10 to 12

Myra Judd

INDEX

O

Orange

P

Passover

Pasta

Congregation Beth Shalom Sisterhood
5915 Beacon Street
Pittsburgh, PA 15217

Please send _____ copy(ies)   @ $19.95 each _____

                 Postage and handling   @ $ 3.00 each _____

                                         Total _____

Name _____

Address _____

City _____ State _____ Zip _____

Make checks payable to Beth Shalom Sisterhood.

Congregation Beth Shalom Sisterhood
5915 Beacon Street
Pittsburgh, PA 15217

Please send _____ copy(ies)   @ $19.95 each _____

                 Postage and handling   @ $ 3.00 each _____

                                         Total _____

Name _____

Address _____

City _____ State _____ Zip _____

Make checks payable to Beth Shalom Sisterhood.

Congregation Beth Shalom Sisterhood
5915 Beacon Street
Pittsburgh, PA 15217

Please send _____ copy(ies)   @ $19.95 each _____

                 Postage and handling   @ $ 3.00 each _____

                                         Total _____

Name _____

Address _____

City _____ State _____ Zip _____

Make checks payable to Beth Shalom Sisterhood.